Also by John N. Cole

In Maine
From the Ground Up (with Charles Wing)

STRIPER

12/5/78

for Jim McCrea —
who shares my affection
for the striped bass —

with good wishes —

John Cole

JOHN N. COLE
Drawings by Marvin Kuhn

AN ATLANTIC MONTHLY PRESS BOOK
LITTLE, BROWN AND COMPANY Boston–Toronto

STRIPER

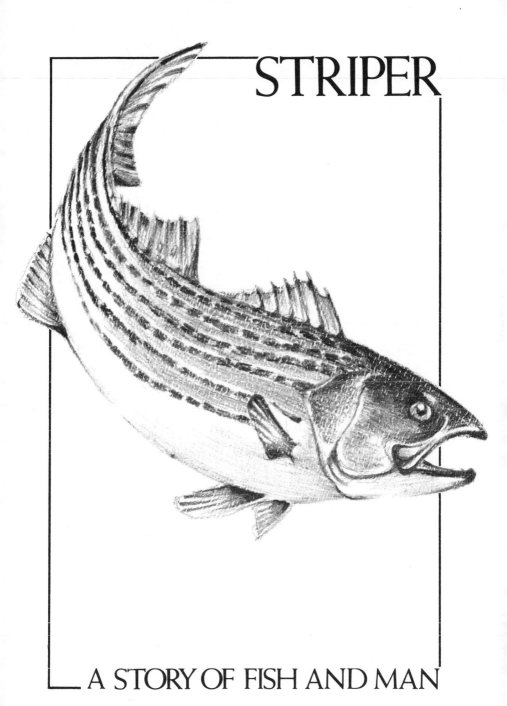

A STORY OF FISH AND MAN

FIRST EDITION

T 11/78

Library of Congress Cataloging in Publication Data

Cole, John N   1923–
    Striper, a story of fish and man.

    1. Striped bass fisheries — New York (State) — Long
Island.   2. Striped bass.   3. Fishermen — New York
(State) — Long Island — Biography.   I. Title.
SH351.B3C64 1978   639'.27'58   78–15003
ISBN 0–316–15108–4

Portions of this book have appeared in *Country Journal.*

ATLANTIC–LITTLE, BROWN BOOKS
ARE PUBLISHED BY
LITTLE, BROWN AND COMPANY
IN ASSOCIATION WITH
THE ATLANTIC MONTHLY PRESS

Designed by Janis Capone

*Published simultaneously in Canada
by Little, Brown & Company (Canada) Limited*

PRINTED IN THE UNITED STATES OF AMERICA

"A North Carolina friend with whom Mr. Lester haulseined, when fishing there was better, drowned last week when the dory in which he was gillnetting turned over in the surf off Ocracoke.

" 'Sometimes it doesn't pay to go out for a handful of fish,' said Mr. Lester, adding that his friend's boat was the only one that ventured out onto the ocean that day."

(From a report by Susan Pollack in the East Hampton Star, 1/19/78)

To Peter C. McKelvey

During my twenty years as a Maine journalist I
have been visited by many young people. Some of them
come seeking counsel, others with ideas for making
Maine, and the planet, a better place to be.

Peter McKelvey was one of those. His concepts of
new ways to encourage wise land use among those who
live on the land were at the heart of a career he pursued
for a short, but intense few years. I helped Peter in
only the most ordinary ways: a bit of office space, a bit
of my time.

On a winter night, more than a year ago now, Peter
McKelvey died long before his time. But his interest in
working for the earth's environmental integrity lived on.
It was through a bequest to me, from Peter, that I found
the wherewithal and the time to write this book — a
book I believe strives for many of the same goals Peter
McKelvey sought.

Peter, I hope I have done well by you. I tried.

STRIPER

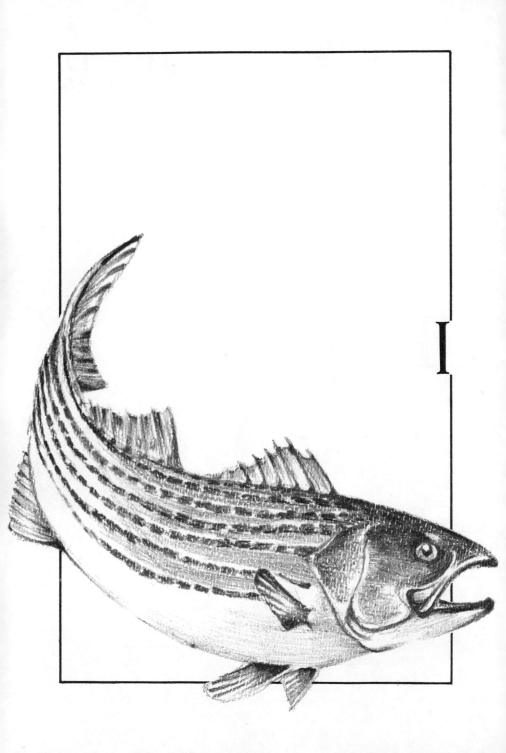

I

There is life here. The river shines with it.

There is death too, both life and death on a scale so extravagant that it clouds human comprehension in the same way the river's turbid waters conceal much of the submerged melodrama.

But there is evidence enough. It surfaces here on the Nanticoke this April morning in milky swirls of milt as white as the pale serpents of fog that trail their chill bellies along the curling river as it winds from the lower Chesapeake, past Roaring Point, past Marshall Point, past Vienna and along Big Creek Marsh where the striped bass have gathered after a journey upriver from the salt sea and the brackish bay to this narrow freshwater reach that is their instinctual coupling bed.

There is light, but the sun is not up. The mist hangs low in the windless dawn; it will not leave until the sun rises over the marshes. When the fog lifts on the new day's first warmth, the sun is spread on the Nanticoke in a silver sheen that glistens the entire length of the river mile from Riverton to Fork Point. The sheen smells heavily sweet; it has a particular, but agreeable, odor.

It is the fragrance of fecundity, a part of the evidence of life that is corroborated by the sheen — a satin film spread by oils in the semen of the male striper, issued with such generosity that it becomes a river within the river, a torrent that stretches from bank to bank and fills the dawn with the perfume of its potency.

All night the bass have coupled here. They have come to this place as they have done since the Indians were the only fishers on the Chesapeake, and before. In the diversity of their spawning journeys, the stripers move toward the headwaters of each of the twenty-one major rivers that nourish this great bay — the continent's largest estuary. But of those rivers, few are more gorged with bass than the Nanticoke, a modest, placid waterway that begins as a Delaware stream, broadens enough to be navigable and useful as an industrial resource, and then crosses the Delaware-Maryland border west of Hawks Neck Shoal. It is below the swinging bridge at Sharptown that the bass begin their sexual congregation, filling the Nanticoke from there to the bridge at Vienna, nearly four miles downstream, with their turbulent presence.

The fish move with the phases of the moon, the time of the tide, the warming of winter waters, the call of migrating wildfowl, the height of the sun at noon, the greening of the marsh grass and a score more seen and unseen changes of the seasonal patterns above and below the surfaces of the Atlantic and the Chesapeake. They move in response to migratory mysteries yet unsolved, yet unknown. The larger females, ponderous with their ripening eggs, bull past or through the gill nets of the Maryland watermen who watch each April for the coming of these silver creatures they call "rock."

Each in his own reach of the river, territories assigned from father to son, from family to family, the watermen drift their nets in the river's currents. There are a dozen spidery barriers afloat between Vienna and Riverton on this April morning; they clog the river passage with the suspended tendrils of their meshes, hung in a lacework from one corked line to another, weighted with small bags of sand, filled precisely so they nudge the river bottom, but do not hold it.

The nets collect their tolls. The bass, for whom the river is a passage toward the preservation of the species, come sliding, silver, over the gunwales of the skiffs. Some, but not all. Even as the twine is raised and tangled fish retrieved, more stripers swim beneath the watermen in a living countercurrent that can not be turned.

As long as a tall man's leg, with backs black-green, sides stitched from gills to tail with seven dusky stripes, and bulging bellies as silver-white as the new moon, some of these brood females, these supple cows, will cast more than a million eggs. Their body cavities swell with their burdens; their drive toward the headwaters becomes a compulsion of such tension that many of these powerful matriarchs rend the nets from cork line to drag line, leaving the waving ends of the torn twine as yet more evidence of the silent drama in this deep.

A thousand of these great fish, gathered off Big Creek Marsh, would be an ordinary Nanticoke event during the spawning surge — a thousand creatures each laying 600,000 eggs. If, as is also ordinary, each of the thousand females is tended by three mature, milt-heavy males, the release of semen and eggs in a few acres of this relatively narrow river can alter the river itself.

On the night before this dawn there must have been tens of thousands of bass, for the water is no longer water, but a fluid so saturated with eggs and semen that the Nanticoke's surface is clogged with their pale presence and the air of this watery Maryland mile is sweet with residues of the stripers' springtime ritual.

There are a billion eggs here. In the hours of darkness, isolated in the privacy of their mutual turmoil, the male-female writhings on the surface which the watermen call "rock fights" have produced a sea of translucent pearls, each about the size of a hummingbird's eye, each patterned with the genetic potential to grow to become as long as a tall man's leg.

The eggs, as a mass in the belly of the bass, are as green as the new spring grass. Extruded in a labor that often prompts the she-bass to push head-to-head against the snout of an attending male, the eggs fall without sound or violence like pale ribbons fluttering in the river's gentle current. He-bass, jostling each other for the privilege, cast their fertilizing sperm in jets of milt, so munificent in its quantity that it glazes entire reaches of the river.

Within the one-celled sphere that is suspended, in turn, within the pale chorion — the thin and flexible shell around the fluid that surrounds the cell — the sperm joins the egg and brings it to life.

Even as the parent fish depart, spent now, riding the river currents to the sea, a cell divides within the tissue spheres they have left behind. As hours pass, more movement within the cell strengthens life's slim thread. In one day, the sphere within a sphere is distorted by the promise of a tail, and soon, what had been a translucent pearl has become a transparent stalk, punctuated at one end with two dark eyes.

Within three days, while millions of its brethren have died unborn within the small universe of their chorion, this cell group becomes a larva — a distorted miniature of the great stripers that spawned it. In a thrusting replica of the survival force that its tail will provide, the organism uses its tail as an infant bird uses its beak, thrashing at the chorion membrane until the sac that held the creature's initial nourishment is ruptured and the fry swims free.

He is one of 600 survivors of the initial 600,000 eggs released by his maternal parent. His arrival at this stage is a result of the exquisite equilibrium of his particular egg and the elements which cradled it. The egg neither sank, nor bobbed to the surface, but circled within the minute dimensions of its own specific gravity, at the whim of the river currents and the uppermost touch of the tides. It was in this vital balance that the fry realized his survival.

He is one of the smallest creatures in the Nanticoke, scarcely larger than the suspended sediments of dying grasses. In their decay, the grasses build the organic base for the microscopic plankton on which the fry must feed if he is to survive. Unless the behavior patterns are in place within the interlocking intelligence systems of this quarter-inch creature, he will not move, open-mouthed, toward the living protein and vegetable matter the plankton constitute.

This much at least have the parent bass done in their selection of the Nanticoke as nursery: in the river's very turbidity, in its delicate mix of tidewater and fresh water is the mechanism for the natural production of plankton on a vast scale. As this fry moves on his own, the tail that beat its way out of the chorion's wall now thrashes to provide the thrust that slides the splinter through the water. And as he wiggles, the smallest bass opens and closes his mouth. He has become a consumer, a taker of sustenance that will fuel his growth. Even as the currents carry the fry past the dead eggs and the dying bodies of his brethren, this one persists in the business of consumption and digestion.

The first twenty-four hours are critical. Provided with enough nourishment from the fluids within the egg for some margin of survival, the fry must utilize this stored energy to launch his search for food — a hunt that will continue for a lifetime. It is death that is common, life that is rare by the time the striper evolves to fry. Of the billions conceived and born, only hundreds remain. The rest are corpses so small that their microscopic skeletons are mere motes — dust hovering in the river water.

In six weeks, the fry has become recognizable as a small fish. His larval lumpiness is gone, his head, torso and tail are impressions of the species; there are no stripes yet on the inch-long creature, swimming now with two other survivors of the brood that began as 600,000. The three have joined others born in the Nanticoke to form a school, swimming in the relative security of a group. They are now large enough to take freshwater shrimp, insect larvae and even an occasional small fish.

Thus they will move through the summer, growing through the July and August days to double their May length. Staying in the shallows, they will edge closer to the open bay.

By the April of the following year, the fish that were parents will move by their unrecognized and unacknowledged offspring, now adolescent bass, striped and longer than a man's hand.

When two Aprils have passed, the eggs of this morning on the Nanticoke will have grown to a foot long. Their histories are sagas of survival. Nourished by the struggle, as well as by their constant consumption of protein, the second-year stripers (on the brink of adulthood) have compressed a vitality within their skins that surpasses the extraordinary.

Men can not become fish, nor can fish transform themselves into men. But over the centuries, men have learned to appreciate in creatures, qualities that are also recognizable in humans. Men who know the striper know it to be a creature of strength and sinew, endowed with a unique determination to survive. Few other fish will attempt the striper's runs and lunges; none have attained the striper's mastery of the surf and the tides — those turbulent inshore presences which other fish avoid, and in which the striper is most itself. Like shafts of muscular light, the striped bass races through the arcs of breaking waves, swirls in the white water of rolling surf, rolls in the tumult of a riptide, somehow finding the power in its broad tail and bronze shoulders to master currents that no other creature can navigate.

If there is a reason for this, the same men who say the striper is courageous and vital also explain that these qualities are the heritage of its dangerous beginnings. From the days of its genesis in the darkness of the swirling Nanticoke, out of the murk of millions of its brothers' drifting skeletons, from the terror of the first hunt, its earliest killings, and the attacks of other predators upon it, the surviving striper emerges with a sinewed heart, a vast capacity for courage, a determined will to live. Having endured so much of the nearness of death, the creature generates an extraordinary exuberance for life.

To have survived, to have endured winter ice, the suffocation of summer's heat, to have somehow avoided the deaths that scattered like grain from a torn sack, these are the searing experiences that provide the pulse to the broad bass tails. From each of the risks run and dangers cleared, has come a full measure of life force — an appreciation of existence that gives these animals the strength to swim, leap, roll, and lunge with a degree of pure energy that surpasses most others.

Consider then the dark forces it would take to extinguish the striper's fires, to end the survival of this most determined survivor. What would be the message for the men who have assigned to this fish the qualities of courage, the virtues of bravery and strength? If this fish were to vanish, how much time would be left to the men who extol it?

These are questions to ponder as the three two-year-old stripers — the legacy of 600,000 — prepare to leave the Chesapeake. Moved, perhaps by the compulsions of their own vital spirits, or perhaps by the drummings of the need to migrate, these fish, this year, will join their parents when April ends and more abandoned eggs cloud the Nanticoke.

Riding the river currents to the sea, they will travel south to Cape Charles where the bay meets the open ocean. From there, the stripers will turn north, creatures of the wild Atlantic now, embarking on an adventure which began on an April night more than fifty miles north in the Nanticoke's milky swirls of milt.

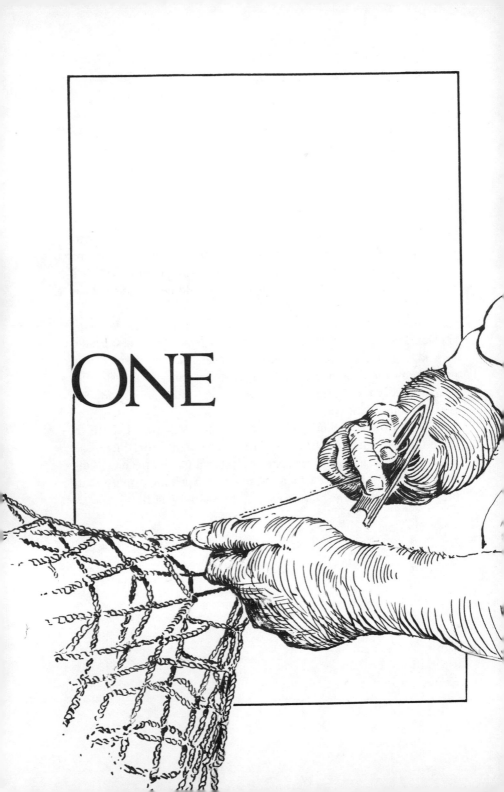

ONE

W here did I learn to row?

How do I know? In the *Emma*, I suppose — the narrow, flat-bottomed rowboat my grandfather bought at Macy's and stuck off the end of the dock at our summer house on the pond, in case any of the house guests wanted to take a spin around the lake in the evening, or Granny wanted a ride to the cove at the far end of the pond where her old, white-haired friend lived in the big stucco house with a red tile roof that looked as if it belonged in Spain instead of on the eastern tip of Long Island.

I found a kind of escape in the *Emma*. (She never had that name officially. That was my grandmother's name and I tagged the rowboat with it because I'd seen women's names on the sterns of commercial fishing boats at Montauk.) Instead of going to the tennis club for tennis lessons, or the beach club for swimming lessons, or the yacht club for sailing lessons, I liked rowing the *Emma* around the lake, poking at snapping turtles, catching blueclaws, tending the eelpots I made with materials charged to the family account at East End Hardware, and every now and then, especially if I could get my brother Chick to help, dragging the *Emma* across the strip of beach at the Gut and launching her in the ocean where we'd row just outside the waves, seeing how close we could come to swamping the old boat in the breakers, horsing around until we sank her. Then we'd drag her ashore, laughing, dump the water and drag her back to the pond before we caught hell from Granny who might be able to see us from her big house on the dunes just up the beach.

"I guess that's where I learned to row," I yell at Jim who's sitting amidships in front of me in the Main Beach dory. Swede is in the stern, leaning back, watching us, his broad ass resting on the narrow ridge at the top of the dory's V-shaped transom. He isn't smiling; he never does, but if he did, he would be now; that's how close he is to it.

I suppose it is a comical sight — Jim and I trying to look like old salts stroking the long, heavy oars when this is our first time ever together in a dory, I on the bow oars and Jim amidships, setting the stroke.

"Keep in time with me, Cap, that's all you have to do. Come on, John, put your back in it."

I try. I try and I wonder why the hell both of us are here in this boat with this man we hardly know, when just a week ago we were in Manhattan, one hundred twenty miles west of here along Long Island's wide, white sandy beach. There isn't anyone I know in this place except Jim, and I don't even understand how we got together. I don't suppose I ever will.

I'd seen him around over the years. Nobody ever forgot the day he buzzed the beach club in his P-40 just before he went to Africa in the war. His cousin Donny was a club beachboy. I knew him a bit. He took care of the sunroom where Chick and I changed into our bathing suits. Chick and I kidded around with Donny, snapping towels, throwing wet ones.

When Jim flew over, Donny told us who he was. I think it was that day that pushed me into the Army Air Force; I joined just before being kicked out of Yale, remembering how great the P-40 had looked roaring over the beach at fifty feet, rolling over the ladies' sunroom — where I imagined Jim could see real naked women instead of the ones I fantasized — and then standing on its tail, climbing straight up, leveling off and wagging its wings in a kind of movie gesture: Jim saying goodbye on his way to war. It was glamorous as hell.

We were both still in uniform four years later when we met one summer night in a Main Street bar. The war was about to end; we were hard drinkers — or trying to be; I threw up most of the time. Jim was a major and I was a tech-sergeant, but we were both combat air crew, so that didn't matter much. That's where we saw each other, I guess, at bars.

Then one winter afternoon the phone rings at the family house on 65th Street in the city and it's Jim. He's in town working for a furniture designer. That's what he learned at Antioch. I'm working as a copy writer for a public relations outfit; that's what I learned when I went back to Yale. We get to seeing more of each other, back in the bars again.

A year or so goes by: I get tossed out by my parents, move in with my grandparents, and Jim and I are seeing each other every few weeks or so, talking about how we don't like the city much, how we don't like our jobs at all, and how we wish we could be back running the Fishers Island Country Club launch as each of us did, a summer apiece, just after college. And finally, this first week in October with the sun spilling over the flinty city streets, we both say the hell with it and quit our jobs and take off for the East End where Jim says he'll put me up with him in the attic of his mother's apartment on the top floor of his Uncle Percy's place on Main Street.

That first day we head straight for the beach to roll in the sand and tell each other how great it is we are here instead of taking shit in some city office. It's the second time I've ever been to the Public Beach — the Main Beach is what it's called by the townies who go there, but my grandmother always calls it the Public Beach the way she always says, "That must be some trades-

man," whenever the back doorbell rings. The only time I was here before was one Fourth of July when Chick and I rode our bikes the two miles along the dune road from our house on the pond to see the fireworks.

There were thousands of people on the beach that night; the moon came up full and red just at dusk and the skyrockets were great. Chick and I sat there on the dunes and we loved it. But we never came back. If we wanted to swim, we went to the Gut, or on the beach in front of my grandparents' house, or at the club, where there was a pool and the ladies' sunroom.

So I'm relieved to come back to the Main Beach in October when the season is over and only a few people are out, sitting far apart, wearing sweaters or keeping towels wrapped around them. As far as I'm concerned, it's the best time of the year. The air is cool and dry, but the sun is bright, and when Jim and I sit in the lee of the beach building out of the northwest wind, it might as well be summer — except for me, it's somehow better than summer because the people have gone and we are being given these days as a kind of bonus because we had the moxie to quit our jobs and get out of the city.

The breeze off the land has got the ocean flattened out. Small, sharp waves are breaking on the beach, instead of rolling in white and foamy from the outer bar the way they often do. We're lying there in the afternoon sun watching Swede, the Main Beach lifeguard, rowing the beach dory in back of the surf, getting ready to set his gill net. Jim tells me how it works.

"There's an anchor on the inshore end tied to a rope bridle, and that's tied to the cork line and the lead line — top and bottom. The anchor goes out of the boat first, then the bridle, then the net. It's about three hundred feet long — that's fifty fathoms, Cap — and about fifteen feet deep. It hangs there, just like a curtain. The corks keep the top line up, the lead weights keep the bottom down. The offshore end is anchored too, so the whole thing stays straight."

"But how does it catch fish, just hanging there?"

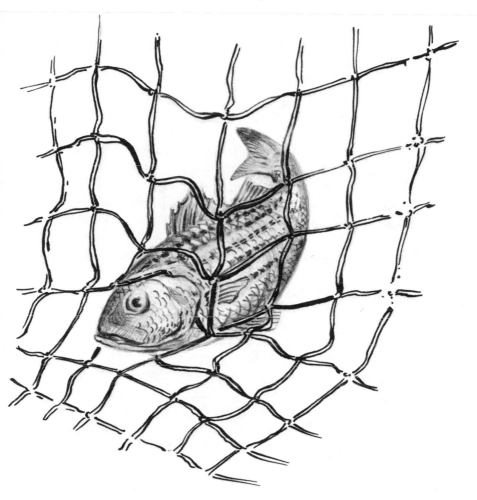

"They swim into it, Cap. The bass like to fool around just in back of the surf. They come close inshore at night to feed.

"That net stretches from the top of the water to just off the bottom. Fish swims along, doesn't see the twine, drives his nose and his head right through one of those meshes. That's the reason for the diamond shape: it fits the fish. Swede's nets have a three-inch mesh, just right for five- to ten-pound bass — the ones that are the easiest to handle, and bring the best money.

"While you're sleeping, John, the bass comes along, pushes his nose through the meshes until he's stuck. He can't back out because his gills flare too much. He just hangs there, thrashing around, waiting for you to come back the next morning, lift the net and yank him out.

"Slick as whale shit, ain't it Cap. Working for you while you sleep."

"How'd you learn so much?"

"Talking to Swede, hanging around. There's a lot of East Enders who keep a gill net or two in their yard. Slap it right in there when they get the word the fish are moving. Get a hundred pounds at thirty cents a pound, that's thirty bucks you didn't have when you went to bed."

Swede is standing up in the dory now, ready to heave the offshore anchor. The northwest wind helps him make his set; the line of corks along the top of the twine is dead straight, perpendicular to the beach. He flips over an anchor with a line tied to one of the flukes; the other end of the line runs to a flag buoy, which is the last thing Swede tosses. The flag stick, weighted at the bottom with corks around its middle, sits straight up in the water, and the red bandanna tacked to its top flutters in the afternoon breeze. The flag and corks are the only indicators of all the gear that's out of sight underwater. I wonder if a fish has already hit the net and gotten stuck in it.

Jim stands up, brushing off the sand. "Let's give him a hand," he says and starts walking toward the surf. Swede is still standing facing the bow, rowing standing up the way I'd seen it done in movies like *Captains Courageous*. When he gets the dory just in back of the breaking waves, he slows almost to a stop, looks behind at the horizon. A couple of waves slide underneath him, moving the dory up and then dropping her down. Then, when there is a pause in the rhythm of the waves, Swede rows like hell. The dory moves just in back of a breaking sea and skids onto the hard, brown sand where the waves peter out in just an inch or so of wash.

Swede jumps out, grabs the bow of the dory, trying to pull her up the inclined beach. Jim grabs on and pulls too; then me, wetting my shoes in the wash. The dory is much heavier than she looks bobbing around on the ocean. A larger wave breaks. The wash is deeper, and when it starts to slide back down the beach I'm afraid the dory is going to go with the undertow.

"Hang on," says Swede, "I'll get a roller." He scoots up the beach a ways, brings back a round, slatted roller, kicks it under the bow, and once we get the dory moving up onto the shore, she goes much more easily.

We're puffing when we get her up onto the level beach where the sand is soft, white, and difficult to walk in. Swede keeps picking up the roller when it comes out from under the stern and carrying it to the bow so we can push and pull one more time. He doesn't stop until we have the dory almost touching the edge of the long porch that wanders along the front of the rambling, gray-shingled building that houses the Main Beach office, snack bar, supply storehouse, men's and women's bathrooms, sunrooms, changing lockers, and — on the second floor of the steep-sided, shingled tower that ends in a flag pole — a small, two-room apartment where Swede lives all year round.

"Thanks," he says after we get where we're going. His thick, bare, tanned legs are still wet; he's wearing bathing trunks and an old, sleeveless sweat shirt over his barrel chest. His hair is blond and his eyes blue, like those of a Swede on a travel poster; but he is bigger and stronger than most men, and he's not puffing nearly as hard as I am.

He puzzles me, though, with his silence. I sense a sadness about him, a loneliness that fits with this nearly deserted summer place where the wind blows sand over the wooden walks and chills the stragglers leaving the beach now that the October sun is low in the west and the evening is coming on.

Swede is on the stern, looking out to sea, giving orders. "Get in, John." I climb over the side, sit in the bow seat, push the oars out through the tholepins so I can row, even though the water is too shallow for the oars to bite. I turn to peer over my shoulder, watching for big waves.

"Keep your eyes in the boat," Swede says. "Looking around that way can get you in trouble. You may not be ready to row. You may hesitate when I say go, and we'll miss our chance, or worse, if there's a heavy sea on."

I turn around, trying to see in Swede's eyes what he can see over my shoulders. I want to watch the waves with him, but I don't want to screw up or act scared this first morning.

Jim gets the word from Swede to get in; he climbs over the gunwales and sits right in front of me, amidships. He puts his oars out, saying nothing, and we both wait for Swede's next move. He's back there, looking off to the horizon. I think he's a bit too dramatic about the whole moment; it isn't that rough.

Then he yells, "OK, pull," and starts pushing hard on the stern. "Come on, pull you guys!"

We're moving faster now. Swede's up to his waist in the water, then he grunts and climbs in over the stern. "Keep pulling," he yells, and Jim and I stroke hard, keeping in some kind of time until, almost before we know it, we've got the dory in back of the breaking waves. We're on the open Atlantic where we can feel the swells. We stroke more easily, and the dory glides along on the smooth sea.

"Where did you learn to row Cap?" Jim asks as we head for the flag buoy.

As we pass the cork line, I notice breaks in the regular spacing of the round cork floats that hold it up. Swede likes what he sees. "Look, some of the corks are down. We got a few fish in here anyway."

When we reach the flag buoy, Swede gets his hands on the rope bridle, hauls us along it until we reach the twine. Then he maneuvers us, pulling on the net, so the dory is crossways to it.

With the cork line and lead line both in his hands, Swede begins pulling us along the net, toward shore, so that the net comes over the rail of the dory on one side and then drops back into the water on the other.

Swede sees the first fish before it reaches the boat. It is a pale presence in the green water. "Here comes one. Here comes the first one."

He leans out over the gunwale, tipping the dory so the rail is down close to the water, and swings the fish in. It's stuck in the meshes, just the way Jim said it would be. The four strands of twine are pulled taut around it just behind the gills. The fish is dead, has started to stiffen. Swede puts the thumb and forefinger of one hand in the striper's eye sockets, holds the twine with the other hand and yanks the fish through the meshes, squeezing it so hard that stuff oozes out of its asshole. He drops the fish in the dory; it thumps on the deck more heavily than I had imagined it would, and I look at it down there by my feet — the first bass I've seen taken from a net. The sun has just come up and the wet side of the fish catches the new light.

Swede keeps on hauling on the net, slowly, carefully. He doesn't want any sudden moves to shake out fish that may not be gilled tightly enough. There are crabs along the bottom part of the twine near the lead line. When they reach the gunwale Swede stops hauling. He reaches for a kind of billy club he has made from the top of a broken oar and bashes the crab against the rail with it, then shakes the pieces of shell and the bright orange guts out of the twine so that they fall back into the sea. I watch the shards of shell drifting toward the bottom like snowflakes, white in the morning light, sinking slowly until I can't see them in the dark green of the ocean.

There isn't too much for me and Jim to do except to watch Swede work the net. It's a still, clear autumn morning, and the sun is now high enough to warm our backs. We are far enough offshore so I can see a whole sweep of beach. Two miles to the west are the white chimneys of my grandparents' house on the dunes, rising from the gray-shingled roof and catching the sun-light. In the October clarity, the place looks close, yet I realize how far I have traveled, and how little, in the twenty-five sum-mers since my first memory of this Atlantic.

It was one of the maids who tossed me in; she was Finnish I think. There was a houseful of servants: Hilda the lanky cook, Lydia the pantry maid, then the upstairs maids, from the same Finland town, as far as anyone could tell. And there was a dress-maker, a gardener, and Cadden the chauffeur, who hid bootleg whiskey in the trunk of my grandfather's Packard so he could make a little on the side when he drove my grandparents to the city.

The maids would take me to the beach every sunny afternoon. "Get the baby wet, Lydia, get some salt water on him."

Strong, brown hands reached for me; I heard giggling as I was held high, naked, white, plump. Lydia trotted with me across white sand that was so hot in the July sun that it would burn her bare feet if she stood still too long. At the edge of the sea the sand was tan, wet and cool; I felt the coolness of the air as I was swung down, held over the white water foaming under me.

The hands let go. I dropped, trying to stand under the curl of a breaking sea. I saw the silver bolt of the sun's reflection rocket-ing along the curving wall of the wave. As the wall arched and began to fall, the sunbeam slithered like mercury along the ceiling of my collapsing tunnel. The roof fell in, the light left. My world was green, turbulent and roaring as I tumbled to the sand and swirled in its grainy presence.

The hands grabbed me close under my arms and hoisted me from the foam. Lydia shrieked and held me high over her head. Blinking the brine from my eyes, I saw the sun shining on those white chimneys.

Swede spots another gilled fish. I realize there could have been bass in that wave with me. They swim close enough to shore.

"Shit," Swede says, "This fish must have hit yesterday afternoon. The sand fleas and crabs have got it." He yanks out a bleached remnant of what was a striper; its guts and eyes are eaten away, and the flesh on its back is tattered as if it had been dipped in acid. Swede flips it over the side.

"That's why nets have to be tended early. If a fish dies in the twine, crabs crawl up, and fleas swim up and are on it almost right away. Sometimes they get so bad, it don't pay to set.

"Now here comes a good one."

This striper is larger than the others, caught by the protruding angle where its upper and lower jawbones join. It could not drive far enough into the net to jam its gills and suffocate, and it thrashes with its tail and rolls its body as Swede hauls it carefully nearer the gunwale. He slips it over the rail, still tangled in the twine, frees it and it drops to the bottom, splashing the inch or so of water in the bilge as it beats its tail on the dory deck. We have seven bass now.

Except for the sea robins and an occasional menhaden, the

stripers are the only fish in the net. Swede doesn't like the brown,
box-headed, spiky robins. He has to work too carefully to avoid
being pricked by the spines that protrude from their heads, back
and gill plates.

"Goddamn little fish, I don't know how they get so tangled."
The robin croaks hoarsely as Swede picks at the twine around its
head; the fish sounds like a bullfrog in pain. When it's clear,
Swede tosses it high in the air like a ball; the robin twitches its
stubby tail as it flies and splashes into the ocean.

"Cut off their tail section and skin it and you've got a good
fish for a chowder," Swede tells us as he works on yet another. "You
wouldn't think anything so God awful ugly would be good to eat,
but there's nothing that comes out of this ocean that isn't good to
eat if you know how to fix it."

There are fourteen bass in the dory when we reach the inshore end of the twine. Swede drops it back into the water.

"Work," says Jim to the net as we turn the dory for the
beach and start stroking on the oars; the dead fish move with our
rhythm, sloshing back and forth in the bilge water.

By the time we get the dory hauled back to her place by the
Main Beach building, the clock says a little after 7:30 — what I
would call early morning if I were still in the city, yet I'm already
tired. Swede stuffs the bass into two worn-looking bushel baskets
and we carry them upstairs to the sink in one corner of his quarters. The beach sand mixes with their coating of slime and sticks
like glue, hiding the silver bellies, the golden eyes and the dark
stripes. Swede works hard at washing it off. "If you don't get the
sand off, it dulls your knife real quick.

"Now then, this is how you get your fillet." He takes a bass,
puts it flat on the wooden sink counter with the head in his left
hand and the belly toward his own. He cuts just in back of the
head, down along the gill plates, along the belly, through the anus
and on to the tail, poking the blade in so it slides along the bone.
The board is already bloody.

He cuts down the back to the tail, then works the knife along the bones, pulling the meat away gently with his fingers. "Bass have a rib cage. That's the hardest part. You have to cut carefully around the ribs, not through them, otherwise there'll be bones in the fillet."

He gets the side of the fish off, turns the bass over and does the same to the other side. He flips a fillet, skin side down, on the board, works his knife between the skin and the meat, gives a tug, and zip, off comes the skin.

He holds the ten-inch-long strip of meat, about as wide as his hand, up against the window. The flesh is almost translucent. "There, slick as shit. We ought to get three bucks for a pair of these.

"Here, you try it John."

An hour later Jim and I are spotted with blood and fish scales, embarrassed at how awkward we have seemed, and how ragged our fillets appear. The baskets are full of the stripped bass carcasses. Swede is washing and drying the fillets, wrapping them in wax paper.

"I can sell these to Rudy at the market. We might get more door-to-door, but it ain't worth the trouble. I figure there's about twenty-five bucks worth here from Rudy."

Jim looks at me and I look at him. We're both thinking that if we had a net apiece, we could be making twenty-five bucks a day.

"We'll come back tomorrow morning, OK?" he asks.

"OK," says Swede, "if the weather holds."

"Maybe I can get another net somewhere," Jim says. "I think my Uncle George has one."

"Bring it along if you want. I don't mind. You guys can set it if you want. Might as well, there ain't much time."

That puzzles me. "What do you mean, there isn't much time?"

"Well, the bass will be gone by come Thanksgiving. Gone south. And the weather's going to get worse. Probably won't be more than ten days or so that will be good for gillnetting between now and then. You'll have to be some lucky to make a dollar."

"What do we do after Thanksgiving?"

"I don't know, Cap," says Jim, looking at me with that long, hard, blue-eyed look I'll get to know so well. "We'll have to find some way to make a living."

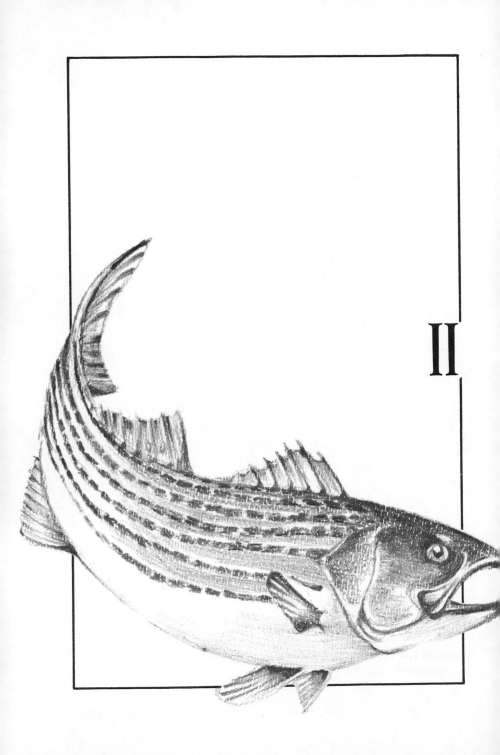

II

In the striper's beginning was the glacier.

It came, a great, ponderous ice plain, one hundred thousand years ago. Moving south from what is now Labrador, the vast sheet slid as slowly as the centuries. Like a hatch cover closing, it obliterated lakes, rivers, forests and all the earth as far south as the mouth of the Hudson River.

In the tumult of its melting and recession 15,000 years ago, the glacier gouged new seas, cut new waterways, mixed the brine of the Atlantic with the pure fresh waters of inland lakes and rivers. From this massive, disordered and traumatic crumbling of natural barriers, the striped bass evolved: a freshwater creature who found a new environment in the channels the glaciers had gouged to the salt sea.

That heritage has shaped the striper's behavior. Since its violent genesis, the creature has never lost its affinity for the purity of its beginnings. Stripers are seldom, if ever, seen more than three miles off the coast; they swim up rivers with the ease of their distant forebears; they select the fresh waters of their ancient ancestors for their most critical rite — reproduction and the preservation of the species.

It was this compulsion that first brought the fish to man. Before Christ was born, East Coast Indian tribes could find the striper spawning in shallow rivers flowing by spring campgrounds. There are records in shell heaps and other archaeological detritus that indicate the waterway tribes knew of the creature; and early in the seventeenth century, with the coming of the European explorers to the New World's Atlantic coast, written documentation of the striper's abundance is duly recorded by the captains, historians and journal keepers who took detailed notes on whatever novel species were discovered, particularly if they appeared to be of value.

The fish is a sort of white salmon, which is of very good flavor and quite as large; it has white scales; the heads are so full of fat that in some there are two or three spoonfuls, so that there is good eating for one who is fond of picking heads. It seems the fish makes the Indians lascivious, for it is often observed that those who have caught any when they have gone fishing have given them, on their return, to their women, who look for them anxiously. [*Isaak De Rasieres, a Dutch commercial agent on the Hudson River, 1623.*]

The Basse is an excellent Fish, both fresh & salte, one hundred wherof salted (at market) have yielded five pounds (sterling). They are so large, the head of one will give a good eater a dinner, & for daintinesse of diet they excell the Marybones of Beefe. There are such multitudes that I have seene stopped in the river close adjoining to my house with a sands at one tyde so many as will loade a ship of 100 tonnes. I myselfe at the turning of the tyde have seene such multitudes passe out of a pounde that it seemed to me that one mighte go over their backs drishod. [*Capt. John Smith, off the New England coast, 1614.*]

The basse is one of the best fishes in the Country, and though men are soon wearied with other fish, yet are they never with basse. It is a delicate, fine, fat fast fish ... sweet and good, pleasant to the pallat and wholesome to the stomach .... When they use to tide in an out of the rivers and creeks the English at the top of high water do crosse the creek with long seanes or bass nets which stop the fish; and the water ebbing from them, they are left on dry ground, sometimes two or three thousand at set, which are salted up against winter, or distributed to such as have present occasion either to spend them in their homes or use them for their grounds. [*William Wood*, New England Prospect, *1634.*]

The maize growers and squash planters of seventeenth century New England were allowed to continue using striped bass as fertilizer for "their grounds" for just five years after 1634. Recognizing the commercial and food value of the fish, the General Court of the Massachusetts Bay Colony issued an order in 1639 which prohibited that practice.

Thirty years later, the patriarchs of Plymouth Colony decreed that funds from the sale of striped bass be used to construct the first public schools in North America. Thus, more than a century before the United States declared its independence the presence of the striped bass had become a bright and significant thread in the American tapestry. So admired was the creature from the very earliest days that in 1879 a sprightly and ingenious public servant named Harry W. Mason spent ten days in June on the Navesink River in New Jersey trying to collect a significant number of striped bass fry for his boss Livingston Stone, the United States Commissioner of Fish and Fisheries.

It was Commissioner Stone's purpose to respond to a plea from his state counterpart in California, S. R. Throckmorton, chairman of that state's fish commission. Throckmorton had discovered the striper on a trip east; he urged Stone to try to transplant some to the West Coast, and Stone dispatched Mason to the Navesink.

"On reaching Red Bank," writes Mason in a subsequent report to his chief, "I found none of the arrangements which we had directed to be made had been attended to; the two men — I cannot say fishermen — had but a faint notion of what was wanted, and had provided themselves with an eel seine wholly insufficient for my use."

Overcoming these nineteenth century bureaucratic barriers with a dogged zeal, Mason got his two "men" to haul a bass seine every high tide around the clock (midnight included) for a week. He and his unwilling crew went to the upper reaches of the river, and . . . "also spent Saturday morning exploring the mysteries of mud and water in every ditch and brook that empties into or communicates with the Navesink River above Red Bank." He continues:

The hauling was continued Wednesday, but as I had sixty small bass, 3½ to 4½ inches long, and thirty medium-sized bass, 6 to 8 inches long, I thought best to be sure of keeping some of them alive, at least, and so staid myself with the fish on the shore for the first time, the men going out alone with an empty tank and a thermometer. As might have been expected, they made a large haul of 139, mostly small, and lost all but twelve before getting back to the wharf. This rather disheartened them, but after considerable argument they were persuaded to try again Thursday, and very fortunately in the first haul we took seventy-five small bass and six large, and succeeded in bringing every one safe to the tank. The tanks were thoroughly washed and filled with water, half from the river, high tide, and half from a spring with sea salt added.

Thursday noon took the train from Red Bank, the tanks being expressed to Grand Central depot, charge, $15. A large truck and three men from Adams Express Company met the train from Jersey City, and at five o'clock the tanks arrived at Grand Central, and on examination only one dead bass was found.

Finding the baggage car was run through Chicago without

change I made arrangements to have the tanks taken in that car, discharged the boy I had brought from Red Bank to help, and congratulated myself that I had one hundred and thirty-three small bass and thirty-four medium-sized bass alive and in good condition. The trip to Albany was uneventful, and with the delivery of the fish I gladly relieved myself of the responsibility that had weighed rather too heavily for comfort upon me during the ten days of my service.

The difficulty in obtaining the bass, requiring the services of from four to eight men day and night for a week made the expense of my experiments more than it would have been under more favorable circumstances (as a week later in time), but I did not dare relinquish in the least particular lest I should lose all the fish I had, and leaving the account to speak for its own necessity I respectfully submit this report of my ten days at Red Bank.

Mason may have worried about the reception given to his expense account, but he shouldn't have. In terms of public monies invested, his ten days at Red Bank and the care he bestowed on his small charges can surely rank as one of the most rewarding projects the U.S. Government ever executed. Of the original Mason group, one hundred seven stripers survived the transcontinental rail journey and were released in the Carquinez Straits near San Francisco. Twenty years later, the West Coast commercial catch of the progeny of Mason's travelers topped one million pounds of striped bass a year. Today, after passage of West Coast laws which prohibit netting, the bass ranges from San Diego County to Vancouver.

The creature that originally surged through the tumult of the glacier's wake to adapt to the East Coast salt sea had successfully survived the man-made tumult of a three-thousand-mile train trip in 1879, and adapted to Pacific waters as well. This is evidently a creature committed to survival.

And well equipped for it too. The striper is strong, muscular, hardy, and — in a marvelous evolutionary metamorphosis — better able than any other fish to cope with the thumping chaos of breaking surf. Hard headed, its gill plates covered with bony protection (plus a set of cutting gills), and blessed with a tail that can be extended laterally to become almost as broad as the broadest part of its body, the striper sports at the foaming fringes of the sea as a mountain goat leaps from peak to peak, or a gibbon swings from branch to branch high above a jungle floor.

Whenever the southeast wind has cleared the south-facing Atlantic beaches of the northeast — especially those in Massachusetts and on Long Island — bass can be seen in the very curve of a cresting wave. Driving smaller bait fish into the white water where the minnows become confused and unable to maintain equilibrium in the surge, the striper feeds easily in the scattering panic, maneuvering gracefully in water so shallow that the fish's bronze shoulders gleam above the pale foam. The striper never loses its composure in its high-risk environment. Often, when a wave's backwash leaves it almost high and dry, the fish will lie calmly on its side in the slight depression between two sand ridges, waiting in the two inches of sea water for the next incoming wave to bring it enough watery space to swim in.

The sight of a four-foot fish weighing close to fifty pounds, on its side in the shallow wash of the Atlantic, startles and amazes most observers. What few of them are likely to realize is the depth of the creature's experience. Bass that size are at least twenty years old, more likely twenty-five. The fish live relatively long lives, even when that longevity is measured on a human scale. Stripers weighing more than one hundred pounds — and catch records over the years are dotted with such giants — are between forty and fifty years old.

On both east and west coasts, the great striper populations spend much of these long lives on their migratory journeys. Vast numbers of the fish follow coastal geography in and out of estuaries, up and down rivers and streams, through natural and man-made tidal channels and canals, around the rims of bays and harbors, and, with conquering vitality, through the swells, riptides, undertows, foaming breakers and surging seas of that most violent place where ocean and land come together.

That meeting line, if every convolution of its granite and sand could be straightened, would cover tens of thousands of miles. The striper is a presence along every one of them, from the St. John River in easternmost Maine to Florida's bather-burdened Atlantic beaches. The striper concentrations, however — the teeming schools which had Captain John Smith believing he could walk "drishod" on their backs — range from the Chesapeake Bay's southern gateway at Cape Charles to the northernmost harbors of Massachusetts at Plum Island and Newburyport. It is between these points that most of the bass move each spring and fall, originating in the Chesapeake each April when the fish move north to return again in December for a somnolent winter in the bay's deeper reaches.

It is a journey that moves them past the great industrial sprawls of the most heavily populated, the richest, the most developed and electrified coastal corridor anywhere on the globe. Past Norfolk, Richmond, Washington, Baltimore, Wilmington, Philadelphia, Trenton, Newark, New York, Bridgeport, New Haven, Providence, Boston and Lynn they go — past more than fifty million humans working in more than ten thousand factories, living in more than twenty-five million housing units, and persuaded that the American Dream is woven from threads of mass production, mass consumption and mass waste, persuaded that the pursuit of happiness demands a compulsive dedication to weekend recreation, and millions believing there are good reasons why fishing is the nation's number one leisure time activity. Many of these spend the work week in factory, store or office, restaurant, supermarket or carwash so they can afford to purchase the rods and reels and lines and boats and boots that will enable them to better catch the striped bass — a creature embattled by the very lunge to industrialism which makes leisure possible for the legions of blue-collar and white-collar and mink-collar humans who have made the striper their favorite fish because it dependably stays within reach, keeps to a seasonal schedule and possesses such a driving life force that it has been caught in city sewers by Manhattan fishermen who lower lines through manhole gratings knowing before they do that they will never be able to retrieve the fish they hook from the fouled, piped waters that run where brooks once ran when stripers swam past the tents of the Algonquin Indians.

No one is certain of all the reasons for the annual journey north from the Chesapeake and back. While the striper population of the Hudson River also migrates, most fisheries biologists, and observers of the river such as author Robert H. Boyle estimate the proportion that migrate from the Hudson at somewhere between ten and twenty percent, and those do not travel with the great sweep of their Chesapeake brethren. The former move only from the river mouth to either Long Island Sound or Montauk Point via the ocean route. If the wintering stripers in the Chesapeake were sealed in that bay by nets at Cape Charles and across the Chesapeake and Delaware Canal, the megalopolistic millions would be denied their favorite sport.

Is it the tides of the creature's evolution that pull it on its voyage? Surely, in addition to its search for food, those currents of past eons must be part of the reason. Like travelers from another country searching for their birthplace in a distant nation, the stripers could be trying to retrace that first journey that began with the glacier's elemental convulsions. The erratic history of the creature's scientific nomenclature is evidence that some ichthyologists share this thesis. Originally christened *Roccus lineatus* (Latin doggerel for the coastal rocks the fish prefers and for the lines, or stripes, that mark it) the bass had its name changed in the 1930s to *Roccus saxatilis* (a redundancy that means rocks found among the rocks) when it was learned that *Roccus lineatus* was a name previously bestowed on a Mediterranean fish that was no relation. Then in 1967, after what has been labeled "considerable research," the striper became *Morone saxatilis* in the wake of pronouncements by the British Museum that the genus *Morone* more accurately indicated the striper's ties to the freshwater perch — the evolutionary progenitor who, with the help of the Ice Age, was probably the genetic parent of the fish that now swims the Atlantic coast twice a year in its search for a homeland that lies buried beneath megatons of glacial till, or under lakes the striper would have to cross mountains to reach.

The price in its numbers the adult striper has paid for its migratory compulsion is a price beyond counting. Who can guess how many thousands of stripers were trapped and speared by hunters of the Atlantic Indian tribes, eager to ease the winter's yearning for fresh meat with the flesh of this large creature that finned slowly through salt marsh channels, or rolled in the shallows of narrow rivers, intent only on its spawning rituals?

Who can ever measure the numbers that were taken by the English and the Dutch and the Spanish and the Italian fleets that made landfall in the New World only to find those harbors writhing with the silver-sided splashings of stripers chasing herring or shrimp? And will there ever be any counting of the stripers stop netted in tidal coves, their gleaming carcasses soiled on the mud flats of their final thrashing after the ebb had left them by the thousands for colonial farmers to hoist to handbarrows for their trip to the corn fields and their burial there?

And, as the nation grew, who ever tallied the bass taken by a growing commercial fishing effort that utilized hand lines, trot lines, line trawls, gill nets, stake nets, drift nets, runaround nets, seine nets, fyke nets, pound nets, trawl nets, scoop nets, trammel nets, and bag nets specially made to be slid under a river's winter ice to trap the bass as they crowded in giant schools near the bottom where the specific salinity and the water temperature were just at the brink of survival limits, nearly cold enough to crystallize the creatures' blood?

And who has ever conceived of a system that would tabulate

the depredations of two centuries of recreational, sport, and meat fishing by individuals using hand lines fashioned from packing string or silk, rods from hickory branches or Calcutta cane; fishing from fifty-foot motor cruisers or wading in the surf; casting Atom plugs, bucktails, tin squid, cedar jigs, live eels, plastic worms, Mooselook wobblers; or trolling umbrella rigs, Japanese feathers and Rebel minnows; or drifting live eels, menhaden, mackerel or a soft-shelled crab tied to the hook with elastic thread?

No, there is no way the fare charged the striper for its annual trips can ever be computed. Every fish taken becomes a river of fish, then a cataract of billions, cascading over the centuries in a torrent of silver shapes that roars its testimony to nature's awesome abundance.

In their annual verification of that abundance, mature stripers still leave the rivers around the Chesapeake every spring after they have spawned. Thinned and weakened by the vigor and intensity of their spawning, the fish ease down the rivers, borne as much by the current as by the listless movement of their tails. After the April nights when the rivers gleam with the fecundity of these fish, the stripers depart the Nanticoke, the Choptank, the Wicomico, the Chester, the Pocomoke, the Wye, the Corsica, the Sassafras and fourteen more Chesapeake rivers that are still striper nurseries. On their way, the spent fish are taken by the river's drift netters, but once by those and in the open bay, they are relatively free of harassment by fishermen.

Starved during their spawning, the fish feed as they travel, gathering numbers as they move, segregating into schools according to size and age, establishing the behavior patterns that will set the schools on a compass course — first south to the bay's gateway at Cape Charles, then north along the barrier beaches of Maryland, past the oil refineries and chemical plants of Delaware and New Jersey, then across Sandy Hook and the Hudson delta in the shadow of the Statue of Liberty, and then past Brooklyn, Coney Island, Fire Island and on along the edge of the open At-

lantic to the beaches of eastern Long Island and the oceanic migratory crossroads at Montauk Point where the Atlantic meets Long
Island Sound and Block Island Sound and where twenty or more
species of food fish and game fish gather during the year on their
migratory travels. Of these comings and goings, none is more certain, more regular than the arrival of the striped bass in May.

Movement ripples through Long Island's temperate spring on
land and in the air as well as under the sea. Furred, hibernating
creatures of the woods emerge from their dens; geese, warblers,
wildfowl, shorebirds and the redwing blackbird flock to the
marshes and thickets of this sandy, scrub oak plain. This wind-
scoured island has somehow withstood enough of the pressures of
the city's millions to still provide East End ponds where Canada
geese can rest on their flight from Carolina to Labrador, or where
the golden plover can swing down for a safe pause on their three-
thousand-mile transnational trip from South America.

Yet each year a bit less eastern Long Island marsh remains;
each year one more pond has been drained. Only the Atlantic survives and holds its territory essentially inviolate, and even that is
invaded by behemoth barges carrying the offal of the city so it
can be dumped in the ocean. But if Long Island's fish of May are
deterred by that dumping, it is a sea change not yet understood
or acknowledged by humankind. There are still too many fish for
that.

There are great spring floods of fish, undersea rivers that
overflow their banks. First the herring, the alewives, bluebacks,
and bunkers, the dense fluttering pods of their millions darkening
the waters like oval clouds of blue dye, their nervous, fragile tails
stippling the sea's surface like a squally breeze, the sound of their
placid progress hissing gently like the wake of a sailing ship.

And after the herring come the dogfish, toothless cousins to
the shark — summer dog and spiny dog, gray replicas of shark
shapes, but in such numbers that if ever they should sprout the
teeth and meanness of sharks there would soon be no other fish in

the sea. They glide by Long Island's eastern beaches in May, the bellies of the females stretched with their cargoes of pups, the infant dogfish born complete, dropped swimming by the dozen from their mothers' wombs with a day's supply of food suspended in the yolk at their umbilici — a day, that's all, to learn to hunt, catch and eat.

Under the dogs move skates and rays, flying over the sea bottom on the undulating wings that give such grace to these creatures of whipping tails and ugly, grimacing features set in the pale alabaster of their unseen undersides. And with the rays and skates, nuzzling the same sea floor, are the sea robins, sand crabs, lady crabs, blueclaw crabs, spider crabs, angler fish, scup, sea bass, tautog, ling, sturgeon, and starfish — all of these and more setting the sea in motion with the sustained movements of their May migration.

The inshore Atlantic, the half-mile of breaking, rolling, surging sea between the outer sand bar fashioned by the largest swells and the inner, barrier beach where the land begins, here in this single ribbon of brine, the scale of life becomes overwhelming in the Long Island spring. From the quiet windless dawns to the evenings ruffled by the afternoon's southwest winds, the corridor teems. Small bait fish — the silver-sided spearing and the sardine-sized herring — flash like a silver rain blown from under the sea. Terrified by the approach of an infant dogfish, or panicked by a scup's rush, the dense schools of these finger-length mites take to the air as if they could find safety where they can not breathe.

When the bait schools shatter the surface and spray upwards in the sun they make a sound like the tearing of a cotton sheet. If the feeding fish are persistent, terns and gulls gather screaming in the sky. Then, as the hapless minnows leap from the yawning mouths below, they jump into the scissoring beaks above. But it takes a feeding frenzy to alert entire flocks of birds. More often, the silver showers of bait break here, there, the length of the beach in occasional and random patterns little noted by either bird or human, yet which are overall a daily and nightly part of the spring sea's particular pattern.

It is only when the stripers and the other school fish move that the birds are likely to gather. First come the small bass, then the middle-weights, and finally, the ponderous patriarchs and matriarchs, the thirty, forty, fifty, and sixty pound fish who wait until May is almost gone before they slide past Shinnecock and the Hamptons. With them come the weakfish, bluefish and some of the larger sharks — makos, threshers and hammerheads.

There is an order to the procession. Places are made for all, even the dense and apparently aimless schools of blowfish, packing stupidly just behind the surf even though the conformation of their stubby frames and inadequate tails makes it difficult for them to survive the inshore surging. Somehow they do survive, even though breaking swells are often darkened by cargoes of hundreds of the small creatures tossed in disarray by their own misjudgments.

The bass make no such errors; nor do the blues and weakfish — the primary schooling, toothed, muscular feeders of the inshore territory. These are the mass killers of the silverside, the mullet, the herring, the shrimp, the tinker mackerel, the blueback and the bunker. When a school of three hundred or four hundred stripers receives its simultaneous feeding message from impulses not yet fully deciphered by humankind, the creatures detonate a group frenzy that shatters the water's surface with the violence of an erupting undersea geyser.

Everywhere the bait fish fly, as if some soundless, invisible tornado were sucking them up from beneath the sea. Broad bass tails smash the surface in white welts of foam; the turnings of the feeding fish start scores of swirling whirlpools, each a mark of the consummate energy a fish needs to reverse its course and swerve open-mouthed through the very center of the mass of panic the bait fish school has become. Shredded bits of bunker, spearing or blueback drift to a surface made slick with the released oils of the tiny, dismembered fish. Sea birds scream of the carnage; their coarse signals carry for miles, attracting hundreds, sometimes thousands of their kin. Then the air above becomes part of the tumultuous mass — a sky filled with stripped feathers, the hysterical cry of anxious terns, the hoarser calls of the herring and blackback gulls, all diving, wheeling, hovering and heedless of any approach as they swallow the hapless bait fish whole whenever the prey are driven live from the sea, or pick with their bills at the flesh fragments that rise in the wake of the stripers' feeding rush.

The gluttony ends with the same unity it began. Another coded message stills the sated school, the birds become silent, scatter; just a few stay sitting on the surface, drifting markers on a patch of sea, mobile memorials to the oceanic moment when ten thousand tiny herring were devoured.

The striper school moves on, traveling east to Montauk, guided by the sound of the rolling surf, compelled to continue by voices calling across the Ice Age with urgings that have transcended every fear of net, spear, hook, and trap since the bass first embarked on their journey, before the Indians, before the colonists, before Harry Mason and before Manhattan's millions.

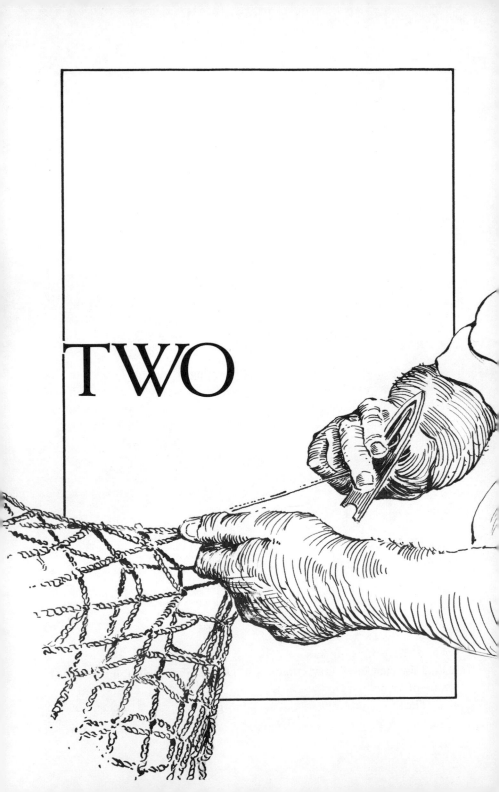

TWO

W e don't know whose woods these are and we don't want to. We are here, sweating in the January cold, thumping axes into the trunks of second-growth oaks, working like hell to cut two cords a day to sell to Jim's Uncle Percy, the town's leading oil, coal, and firewood dealer.

It was all we could think of to do after the gillnetting season ended so miserably. We never did get any nets of our own into the water; the twine we got from Jim's Uncle George had lain so long in a dark corner of George's barn that the cotton fibers had rotted. The net looked great when we pulled it out the barn door and began spreading it over the yard. Then George came out of his potato house in his overalls and walked over to look at the net he hadn't seen for so many years. He picked up a fold, took hold of one bar of one mesh in the fingers of one hand and popped the single strand with scarcely any effort.

"Some tender, ain't it. You won't hold no bass with that." He dropped the twine back to the ground. "I should have hung that net in the rafters instead of throwing it in the corner that way. Good for mackerel now, that's all. Doubt if it would hold too many of them."

There was nothing we could do to get a net after that. There wasn't time. We hung around with Swede, giving him a hand whenever we could. We sold a few fish door-to-door, and he let us keep the money. But there was never much of it, and by the time Thanksgiving had come and gone, Jim and I realized we weren't going to be able to fish for a living the way we had planned.

There were storms late in October, eight days in a row when the surf was too rough to get a dory through it. When we did get a break in the weather, we set the net just in time for a north-easter. That blow was bad enough to tear the net loose from its anchors. We found it miles down the beach at the edge of the surf, rolled into a big, soggy ball, so torn and tangled and clogged with flotsam that it took us another week to untangle and mend it. After that, we were jinxed.

If we waited until afternoon to set the net, the wind breezed up and we couldn't get off. If we set in the morning, trash fish in the net would bring the sand fleas and the next day what few bass we had would be so gnawed we couldn't use them.

One gray dawn after Election Day, the twine froze as it came from the sea. The stiff netting rattled over the gunwale like sticks, and small shards of salt ice slid down the planked sides of the dory.

That was enough for Swede. Instead of hauling the net in over one rail and letting it slide back into the water over the other, he gave a grunt and began gathering the net in his arms, hand over hand, until he could slam an armful on the dory bottom and stomp on it with his boots so the frozen twine would stay down.

"That's all for this year. That's all. Shit, there ain't enough fish here to pay for my coffee, much less you two. I'm putting up the boat and going painting."

Jim and I went wood chopping. Percy never asked where we were getting the oak, so we didn't tell him. We took the Model A and cruised the empty January roads that squirmed through the woods west of the town, beyond the potato fields. We located plenty of woods — enough so we could follow dirt roads and get away from houses, away from people, away from the chance of being found cutting trees on someone else's land. We were so alone out there we could make ourselves believe that no one owned the land, that we were pioneers, taking what we needed off territory we'd discovered just that day.

"Don't ask, Cap. Don't ask." Jim grins and whops his axe into an oak. Percy is paying us fifteen dollars a cord and we try to cut two each day. We tow the first one in on the small trailer when we go back to Jim's for lunch; we try to get a second one in the afternoon. It's not a bad job as far as I'm concerned. When I was at college I spent a summer in Oregon working for a big timber outfit owned by a friend of my mother, so instead of asking Jim how to do this or that, I'm telling him how to set up a tree so it falls where you want it. I've still got the double-bitted axe I bought at the company store. I show Jim how to limb a tree, how to set it up for bucking. It feels good to be able to tell him something instead of listening all the time.

We are bone tired every day by the time it gets so dark we have to leave the woods, and we don't often get that second full cord. But we like the idea of what we are doing. We keep talking about how the work is getting us in shape, about how callused our hands have become, about how tough we are and how healthy the air is.

Cold is the big drawback. The Model A windows won't close; the cab is about rusted out. Jim says we should fix it so we have a warm place to sit, even in the woods. We knock off for two days and build a new cab of plywood, new glass, everything. Jim is a good carpenter — deliberate, careful and concerned about precision. He wants the finished product to look good, and it does.

The new cab is two days old, and we're sitting in it drinking coffee, feeling fine. It's 9:30 and we've already cut most of a cord.

"That's better, isn't it Cap. Just like New York." Jim blows on his coffee and takes a bite out of his banana. Its skin is so brown it's almost black.

"Jesus, Jim, how come you always wait till a banana is rotten before you eat it? Where do you find those things anyway?"

"Tuck 'em away, Cap. Tuck 'em away and wait." He takes a bite. "Ummm, finest kind, Cap, finest kind."

I'm feeling pretty brash after the break. I walk over to a big oak. "Now here's a winner. I can drop this monster right over there, and I'll bet it won't take ten minutes."

Jim pulls out his two-dollar pocket watch, looks hard at the face for awhile, then says, "Go."

I'm jumping around, chopping here, chopping there, knowing I'm not going to have any trouble with the time.

"Five minutes, Cap."

The tree begins to creak a bit in the wind. I can feel it going, and I'm whaling away with the axe. Then, bam, something pops and the oak is coming down. Only it's not falling the way I thought it would.

Crash! The middle limbs land on top of the Model A cab. The driver's side window breaks, the new plywood roof is ripped loose and the driver's side wood frame that Jim spent most of two days joining is fractured in three places.

Jim says nothing. He stands there, looking at his watch, shaking his head. "Eight minutes, thirty seconds, Cap," he yells after a while. He goes over and starts hacking at the limbs, getting the tree ready to buck. For the rest of the winter, we ride around with my side of the Model A in the same sorry condition. I don't talk any more about my time in Oregon.

The sun sets before six through the deep winter, so we have long evenings. We eat early with Jim's mother, sitting in a small kitchen, stoking away platefuls of her cooking. We do the dishes while she goes downstairs and over to the other, larger side of the house to talk with Percy and her sister-in-law.

When we finish, we go into the sitting room and knit twine. Jim thinks we can knit enough to make our own gill net before the bass come back in the spring.

He is stubborn about it. He shames me into doing work that comes so awkwardly to me. He shows me how to load the seine

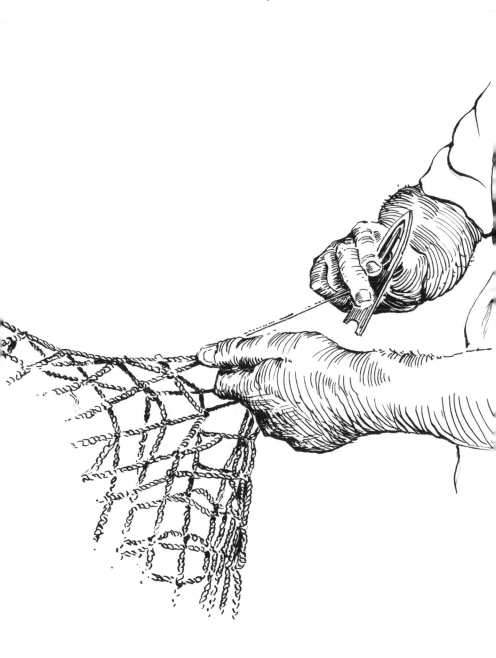

gear. "We'll go back to the Main Beach, Cap. We can work in the sunroom. Plenty of open space there. No one to bother us."

No one but my memories. It wrenches my frame of reference to be working over the same kind of canvas floor-covering that is tacked down at the club — put there so bathers, stripped of their wet swimsuits, can lie naked and splinter-free on the floorboards, shielded from wind and the public eye by the four sides of changing lockers that surround the open central square like the walls of a fort. The Main Beach sunroom is so much the same, I think I'm back at the club, snapping towels, trading jokes with Chick as we run in and out of the showers, tan, lean and resented by the older, paunchier, paler men on their vacations from the city.

I see us running, yet I'm helping Jim tie two lengths of rope from one side of the sunroom to the other; we use the latches on the changing lockers as cleats. The March wind the sunroom's walls can not keep out is raw, but for me summer is still here. Such different lives running their different courses over the same ground, in the same place. And I have lived, am living, both of them.

Pungent with its preservatives, the tarred manila rope comes easily from its coils, cuts across the sunroom in two parallel lines — lines that would block a bather dripping with ocean salt on his way to the shower. On one length of line, Jim strings the corks, brown, round, thick, with one hole drilled in the center of each fat, light disc. They are stripped from the tissues of great oaks growing on the Spanish plains; they come to us wrapped in Spanish burlap, from old fishermen across the sea to young, would-be fishermen on the other side of the same ocean.

So many Spanish corks per so many feet of woven hemp from the Philippines — Jim has figured it from the cork line of his Uncle George's rotted net. He moves along the rope with his measuring stick, placing each cork precisely. Then he strings the opposite rope with the leads — cored weights of soft lead, almost as it comes from the mines. Two six-ounce leads to each cork, spaced just so.

And when the spacing's done, we go to work with the net needles again; this time they're loaded with finer twine and we lash each cork and lead in place, I on one line, Jim on the other, moving with each other, the needles fluttering as they make the triple hitches that hold the corks and leads so trimly in place.

At last the twine we've worked all winter to knit is joined to the two ropes that will give it a shape, a direction, a dimension, a top and a bottom, an up and a down. Each mesh is hung to one-third less than its stretched length, each clove hitch that does the joining is precisely the same distance from every other hitch so that the strain on all the meshes will be equal when a fifteen-pound bass is caught by the bridle and thrashes to break free.

We work through the final March week, across from each other, in step with each other, moving along each length of rope as it is fitted and the net is hung. Once a stretch is complete the ropes are loosed from the locker cleats, the finished length of net is pulled to one side of the sunroom, and the process begins again. We are quiet, Jim with his plans for fishing, me with the laughing, tan and naked ghosts of my summers past around me.

"There, Cap. By Jesus, it's done."

And it is. The net is hung in, the cotton cord fitted with rope, corks, leads, bridles, hanked neatly along one wall, the cork line making the top fat, the lead line coiled flatly at the other side, and in between the net itself, a slim length of twine not much thicker than the oak I dropped on the Model A. I am taken by the handsome aesthetics of the complete net. The dark, tarred rope contrasts with the ivory twine; the tan corks and the dun leads work well with the organic mass. This net could have been woven two thousand years ago; the materials are ageless.

"Grab the leads, Cap. We'll take it home." Jim picks up the cork line, I take the lead line, and we carry the net stretched between us. On our way down the walk we meet Swede, coming home from a day of painting. He's in his overalls, splattered with many colors after his winter of work.

"What's that you got?" he asks, stepping up to the net and reaching his fingers into the twine like a housewife feeling a head of lettuce. "Hank that out on the beach here. Let's see what you two been doing all winter."

We spread the net in neat folds on the windswept sand. It looks in place there, just as Swede's did last October, only ours is whiter, newer, unblemished, unscarred, unused. Swede walks the length of the lead line, fingering every hitch, does the same with the corks, picks up handfuls of twine, looks at the knots.

"You done good. Looks like it ought to work. You got your-selves a dory?"

"No, we don't," says Jim.

"Well I'll tell you, there's a man lives across from where I'm painting. Used to work on a dragger. He's got a smack dory in his yard there — spent most of her time lashed on top of the wheelhouse. One side's worn right through where she rubbed against the mast. Well, she's for sale cheap. You two can make a net like that, you ought to be able to fix up that dory, don't you think, Jim?"

"How much does he want?"

"I don't know. Tell you what, I'll ask tomorrow when I'm down there. Stop by in the evening. I'll let you know. If you want her, I'll throw her on the truck and bring her up here."

We get the word the next day: eighteen dollars is what's wanted for the boat. Jim whips out the money, and the next after-noon, we're back, the only car in the Main Beach parking lot, waiting for Swede to bring us our new boat.

He pulls in, and there she is. The paint is about gone. There is a long, vertical, rounded hole on her port side that looks as if she'd been rubbed with a huge, round rasp that flayed her planks. That's where the mast wore through as she bounced up and down against it whenever the dragger hit hard weather. Jim slides his hand along the dory's bottom that sticks out over the back of the truck.

"Jesus Christ, Swede, she's some flat. All the sheer's been beat out of her." I don't get much of Jim's meaning.

"She'll pull back, Jim. Take a little work is all. Needs a couple of ribs, couple of planks on that side there. Throw on some paint, you won't know her from new." Swede is pulling the dory from the truck. "Come on, give me a hand. Don't want to drop her, do I?" He's smiling; for Swede, it's a big grin.

For the next two weeks, Jim and I work on that dory every day that the weather is half decent, and some days when it isn't. Into the worn planks we bend patches: plywood fastened with brass screws every quarter inch. My hands are blistered from turning the screwdriver. We caulk every seam, replace the rotted gunwales with new oak. We put oak strips along the bottom, new knees at the base of every rib, new thwarts. To me it seems we've taken the skeleton of a dead boat, fitted it with new bones, and then fastened new sinews over those bones. It's difficult to find the old dory under all the patches and replacements we've added.

But the basic form of the boat is still there — the authentic dory lines that give the boat such individuality. We love her for that authenticity. We don't want to be tending an ocean net from some flat-bottom skiff bought off Macy's floor, or out of a tin boat ordered from the pages of a Sears catalog. That wouldn't do for two guys who want to be East End fishermen. The old-timers never go through the surf in anything but a dory or a Jersey skiff — and damn few of those are left.

But Jim is just flip enough to want the dory to be an individual, to make a statement that is brash and humorous, and in its way original. So when the time comes for painting, he buys the brightest blue paint he can find — the sort of blue you might find on a jukebox if they ever decided to paint one blue.

"Come on Cap, slap it to her," he tells me. "We got to get this coat on her before that afternoon wind comes on and blows the sand around. If this paint isn't set by then, we'll have nonskid decks for sure."

I'm down on my knees, brushing on blue paint as fast as I can. The surf is rolling at the edge of the beach. The sound of it has been a constant background to our work on the dory. But as I paint, I keep thinking I hear another sort of sound, a deeper, steadier roaring. Then I'm certain I do. I look up over the dory — turned turtle so we can paint her — and coming down the beach directly at us is one of the biggest, broadest silver trucks I have ever seen.

This truck looks like something off the set of a World War II movie about battles in the Sahara, possibly "The Desert Fox" or "Tobruk." Its wheels are as high as the dory when it pulls alongside and stops. The huge tires are fat; the cab is high above me and Jim as we kneel there, looking up. It still seems high when we get off our knees, waiting to see if the driver has anything to say. We see his lips moving, but it is impossible to pick out the words over the roar of the engine idling in the open air because both sides of the truck's hood are raised, tied up with a piece of twine. Steam hisses from under the radiator cap and we can feel the heat of the motor even though we are several steps away.

Two men stand in the back of the truck, their elbows resting on the roof of the cab that boxes in the driver. Each of the three is wearing the same sort of outfit: chest-high, black rubber waders held up with suspenders pulled over the sort of hooded sweatshirts high school athletes sometimes wear in training sessions. The hoods are down, and at the neck line there are the collars of several shirts showing, each worn over the other. The only difference in the outfits is the choice of caps. The two in the back of the truck wear gray wool, knitted watch caps; the driver has a tan cotton cap with a long, black, pointed visor.

The truck is towing a low, two-wheeled trailer, and on the trailer is a dory that makes ours look like a midget. She's half painted an ugly mustard yellow; her garboard planks are scarred where the trailer tires have rubbed against them. Inside, her deck is littered with sand, bits of crab shell, fish scales, and piled in her stern is a mounded net that looks as large as a haystack. I can't comprehend the scale of a net that makes such a ponderous mound.

Jim and I are standing on tiptoe, trying to look at the twine over the dory's high stern, when a second vehicle comes along the beach out of the east. This is a Model A, fitted with wide tires on its rear wheels; the driver is keeping the wheels on one side in the track made by the big silver truck. When he reaches the bow of the dory sticking off the end of the trailer, the driver stops the chugging Ford, shuts off its engine and he and his rider walk up to talk with the driver of the truck. Both men have the same chest-high waders on; one wears a red shirt and a baseball cap; the other's blond hair pokes out from under the pulled-up hood of his sweatshirt.

The one in the baseball cap puts a booted foot on the truck's running board and yells up to the driver. "See something, did ya?"

The driver shakes his head so the long bill of his cap moves side to side, says something we can't hear, and gestures, jerking his thumb toward our dory. He turns to look at us, and I can see his blue eyes, and a grin on his face. His front teeth are chipped; they are white against the tan of his creased skin and the white-gray stubble of his unshaven cheeks.

The one in the baseball cap, younger, but tan, with a darker stubble and the same water-blue eyes, comes around the front of the truck with his riding mate in the sweat shirt. They walk to our dory, looking at our patch job, and see the net hanked on the beach.

"Gonna try em, are ya?" the one in the baseball cap yells so he can be heard over the truck.

"Guess so," says Jim.

The blond-haired man laughs. His face is long, raw-boned, ruddy, but with the same blue eyes as the two from the Model A.

"By Jesus, you oughtn't go too far in that." He points to our dory. "What are you going to name her? She's a peril, that's what she is. Yes, yes, she's a peril all right. You'd better not let her near

wet sand when she's loaded. She'll suck right to it, she will, bottom as flat as that. How the hell she ever get so flat?"

His mate lifts his baseball cap, scratches his head with the same hand and drops the cap back on. "Ding, you remember that boat. She rode on top of Bill's dragger about twenty years."

"Oh Gawd, is that her. Took some pounding, didn't she. No wonder she's flat." He laughs again. It's a raw-boned laugh, like his face. "Haw Haw." It sounds loud because the truck engine stops, suddenly, and the beach is quiet again. The driver climbs down from the cab. His waders slow his movements as they do for each of the men. He walks up to Jim, looks at him from under the long-billed cap. His eyes are bright, small, like a bird's.

"You Carl's boy?"

Jim nods. "Thought so. Knew Carl when he was punching tickets. I rode them trains once in a while."

He turns and runs his hand along the new gunwale of our dory. I am surprised at how knobby his knuckles are, and impressed with the width of his short fingers. His hands are mottled, scarred, and his fingers close stiffly; they appear to lack the flexibility to grip the gunwale. Both hands look swollen from the wrists down, as if they had been injected with a fluid that had turned hard.

"Gonna try 'em, are ya?" Jim nods again.

"Who's this with ya?"

"City boy," says Jim, "but he's learning."

The blue eyes are on me, peering from under that cap. "He's long enough to row. Put him on the oars. Feed him a beefsteak now and then. Make him horny."

Ding and baseball cap and the two men standing in the back of the truck laugh together. A face we haven't seen appears over the side of the truck body. The man has been lying flat there. He stands, wearing a long, black overcoat over his waders; the coat is buttoned and the collar is up, but the man is bareheaded and nearly bald. The wisps of his gray hair blow like beach grass in the sou'west breeze. "Ted's right. Ted's right." He talks fast, mumbling his words so he is difficult to understand. "Makes you horny as an old goat." He grins, and there are no teeth in his mouth.

"Go back to sleep Smiley," yells Ding. "You wouldn't know what to do with it if you got it up anyway. Ain't that right?"

Smiley grins at me and holds his hands about a yard apart. "If I had a lob like yours, I wouldn't be on this beach. No I wouldn't." He points at Ding, laughing, shaking his finger, nodding his head, stretching his arms out even further and looks up at the sky, rolling his eyes. Everyone laughs but Ding.

"Go back to sleep you old fool," he says, and turning toward the driver of the truck, "come on, Ted, let's go find some fish."

Ted looks at Jim. "Little early, ain't it. Be another week or so yet. But we want to be ready. Who knows, we might come upon a pod before sundown."

He walks toward the truck, stops, turns and says to me and Jim, "Plenty to go 'round. Plenty to go 'round. All we got to do is find them." He climbs up into the cab, the roar starts again, then gets louder as Ding and his driver start the Model A. Ted shifts the truck into gear, the monster lurches forward and the procession rolls off to the west, getting smaller and smaller as it moves along the beach. Smiley stands in the back of the truck in his black overcoat, holding his arms far apart, shaking his head and laughing at Ding, who is sitting in the Model A that's keeping one set of its wheels in the track the big truck tires make in the sand.

When I can't hear the truck anymore, I pick up my paint brush and go back to painting one side of the dory while Jim does the other.

"Well, now you've seen it, Cap," he says looking down the beach at the specks the procession has become.

"Seen what?"

"Seen an ocean seining crew. That's the Poseys. They can get ten thousand pounds of bass in one haul. One hundred boxes. Now that's fishing."

I've finished my painting, wondering why Jim is still at work.

He always outpaints me. I walk to the bow where he's working. He has a small can of powder-blue paint, and he's painting the dory's name with it, over the dark blue of the hull. The name he puts on is *Blue Peril*.

"How do you like that, Cap? 'She's a peril, that's what she is.'" He grins and looks east down the beach. "Who knows? She could take us seining yet, Cap. She could take us seining yet."

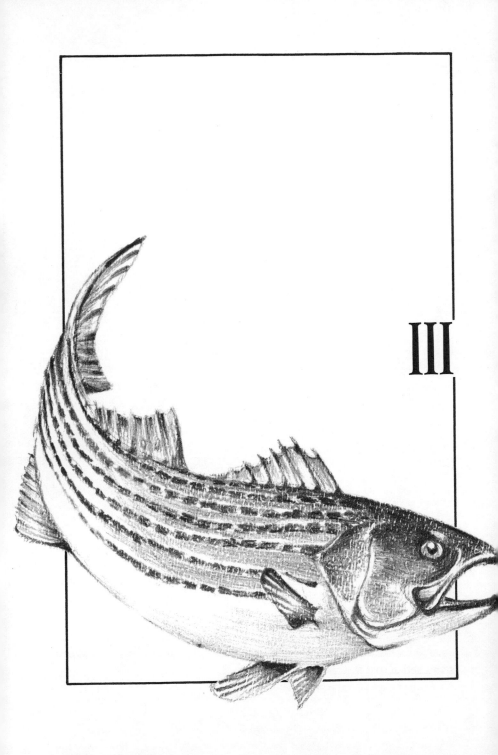

III

W hen the carpenter, Jesus of Nazareth, said to a group of Galilee fishermen, "Let down your nets for a draught . . . " he was advising haul seiners. If today's seining crews could cross the barriers of time to witness the moment, they would immediately recognize the Galilee gear, even though they might have trouble understanding what was miraculous about catching fish in one small part of the sea and not another. Haulseining is like that.

Seines have been a universal piece of fisherman's equipment since the Stone Age. Drawings on cave walls, net-making accessories found in Egyptian tombs, and net artifacts found in the Arctic, Asia and Argentina have set social historians to pondering the ancient transnational communications which moved the net concept so quickly around the world.

The fisherman's bend — the knot which creates each individual mesh and is the soul of the seine — has not been altered or improved since it was first tied by the first net maker. Until the late 1850s, no machine could tie it; every seine made before that date was made by hand, and thousands of miles of twine have stretched across the centuries.

Linen from flax, cotton from cotton bolls, hemp from cannabis, fibers from tropical vines, and silk from silkworms have been converted to the twine from which seines have been knit. Manila ropes run the entire length of both the top and bottom of the long, narrow strip of netting. The ropes support the floats at the top and the weights at the bottom that make the net a vertical wall in the water — an airy wall that flows with the sea, but becomes a prison to every creature too large to escape through the meshes.

The men of Galilee cut floats from cork, cast lead weights for the bottom line. Japanese seiners once blew translucent glass balls so the float lines of their seines looked like wavering strings of emerald beads afloat on an aquamarine sea. Where the smelting of lead had not been mastered, animal skins were filled with rocks and sand, tied in small pouches and lashed to the bottom lines. The suspended weights left their tracks on the sea bottom like so many serpents crawling toward the beach.

Haul seine, drag seine, beach seine — by whatever name, this net can be made by hand from available materials, can be set from small, shallow-draft boats, and hauled back by hand, and requires no machinery of any kind either to make or maintain. The haul seine has produced fish protein for villagers on the Ivory Coast, Eskimos on the Aleutians, and Polynesians on every inhabited island in the Pacific. It is versatile, low cost, rugged and adaptable. It can be sixty feet long or three thousand feet long; it can be set in the Atlantic Ocean or the Sea of Galilee; and not until the twentieth-century advent of steel stern trawlers, super ships of the tuna purse seining fleet and the huge fishing fleets of the eastern European nations has there been, pound for pound, dollar for dollar, a more efficient and effective method for catching the creatures of the sea.

For the striped bass, the haul seine is still the most effective trap. Because the fish frequents shoal waters of the Atlantic coast, because it lives most agreeably in that pale, heaving surf line, the striper is not very vulnerable to fishers of the open ocean, such as beam trawlers and purse seiners. But because it so rarely strays from bays, estuaries, rivers, inlets, and the turbulent rims of the barrier beach, the striper is easy prey for haul seiners who watch and wait for the massive migratory schools just as the Sioux watched for the buffalo and the Eskimo wait for the seal.

So susceptible is the striper to the seine that several states along the eastern seaboard have outlawed netting of any kind. Maryland and Delaware enforce regulations that restrict seining to certain locations, certain seasons and certain striper sizes. Only New York — and that state's access to the sea is restricted to the shores of Long Island — Virginia, and North Carolina still permit relatively unrestricted use of the haul seine, and proposals to prohibit every sort of striped-bass netting are so regularly entered on the legislative agendas in each of these states that they no longer attract attention from anyone but the handful of fishermen who would have to abandon their most ancient and most effective netting techniques.

Those techniques have been considerably advanced since the Nazarene carpenter gave his advice to the fishermen of Galilee. While a haul seining crew from Hatteras or Amagansett would comprehend immediately the gear and the systems employed two thousand years ago, Simon Peter could have no way of understanding the methods used by his counterparts twenty centuries later.

Only the fisherman's bend has not changed — that and the essential shape of the seine. But where the ancient seines were made from materials grown on the land, today's are spun by machines that take the very elements from earth and air and spin them into synthetics with names like nylon and Dacron and monofilament. Other machines spin the synthetic strands into netting — a stiff resilient and incredibly strong web that rides high in the dory's stern, and does not flatten softly like wet linen or cotton.

Nor do the new strands rot like the organic fibers of the past. Luke tells us that Simon Peter's crew were cleaning their nets when the carpenter from Nazareth first passed their way. Before or after every day a seine was set, the net had to be cleaned and hanked out in the air and sun to dry and thus prevent the fiber rot that could begin so quickly with the catalysts of seaweed and fish matter impregnated into cotton and linen lines, damp, dark and warming with the process of decomposition. Until the mid-1950s when the first Dacron and nylon twine came from the steel spinners of the DuPont factories, every fisherman cleaned his nets and dried them, or else he soon had no net — the rotted bars of the meshes would pull apart under the pressure of a stretched thumb and forefinger.

The seiners of the fifties who tried the first synthetics could not accept the incredible notion that cleaning was no longer needed. Stone Age practice had bred traditions too strong to be broken overnight by DuPont. Dutifully they pulled the nylon and the Dacron seines from dories every afternoon, to spread them along the beach to dry. But the younger fishermen, the ones who had grown up with synthetics — with the faith in technology born of mass marketing — laughed at the homage to the ancients and persuaded their stubborn fathers to leave the seines unattended. "Jesus, you got nothing to worry about, Cap, believe me. Try it, for Christ's sake."

And the seines soon stayed in the dory, packed wet, loaded, stomped down with crabs crushed in the meshes, smaller fish left gilled to rot at the center of the seine heap while the synthetic twine spun from earth and air stayed inviolate in its nonbiodegradability.

Then came polyethylene rope to replace the tarred manila hemp that had been the cork line and the lead line for so many centuries. In place of the gold of treated hemp and the fragrance of the tar that came from the new coils, there was the bright yellow, the vivid blue and the novelty red of polyethylene — another synthetic that had no odor of any kind until or unless it was burned, whereupon it melted like wax and stunk of some acrid mystery in its makeup. And on the polyethylene ropes were slipped polyurethane floats, taking the place of the soft corks cut from the living oaks of Spain. The floats too were bright, harsh, hard. Orange Day-Glo, white, red, yellow, black, like carnival balloons inflated to a kind of permanent rigidity, they floated in garish technical proficiency where the hand-blown emerald beads of the Japanese once had been.

Only the lead remains the same. No synthetic weight could be found to take the place of the ancient metal that first oozed from rocks beneath Stone Age fires. The mass that lead contains within the densities of its malleable metal could not be surpassed by the machines of DuPont. The lead weights survive, the same, from Galilee to 'Gansett, but today, polyethylene is spun around a ribbon of lead, and instead of leaden lumps lashed to the bottom line, the line is lead-cored, heavy in its entirety, built for the purpose alone, this and no other.

Until World War II, DuPont, synthetics, and four-wheel drive vehicles designed to do desert battle in the land of Moses, seining's rituals had remained essentially unchanged for centuries. Any boat large enough to hold one oarsman and some twine could be used to set a seine; two men, four men — however many it took to cope with whatever length of net was pulled through the waters of lake, bay, sea or ocean — could do the job by hand, some pulling on the lead line, hand over hand, holding it high to try to keep fish from escaping in a silver leap over the surface barrier.

Piled fold upon orderly fold in the stern of any seaworthy, shallow-draft dory, skiff or sharpie, a seine pays out over the stern like so much coiled rope. If there is a seine setter, the oarsman's work is easier; as he strokes (or they stroke) the net setter casts lengths of coiled lead line over the gunwale as the boat moves through the water. The weights drag the rest of the seine from the stern; the twine falls gently, a curtain adrift until the leads reach bottom. Suspended from its floats, the net wall reaches across an ever lengthening span as the rowers pull, following a crescent course from one starting place on the beach, out into the sea in a gentle, arcing curve until the center of the seine is reached — the pocket, or bunt, woven of the heaviest twine, a net pouch that is the last of the seine to come ashore. Like a boy's marble bag, it holds the catch until the entire, bulging length of it can be hauled to the high beach where the purse string is pulled and the fish slide in a flailing cascade to the sand.

When the bunt goes overboard, tossed by the seine setter in his most skillful and crucial move, it marks the outermost reach of the arc. Oarsmen begin reversing their offshore curve, begin easing back to the beach until the half circle is closed just as the last of the seine slides over the gunwale. A length of hickory stick, the jack, acts as a spreader to keep lead line and cork line separated; from the jack's bridle runs fifty or one hundred fathoms of rope: the link between seine and shore. If the seine has been set in a lake or bay where the surf has no room to build, the line is short; the jack goes overboard close to the beach. In open ocean surf, the jack must go over in back of the breakers, leaving the boat and its men free to concentrate on negotiating the crashing seas. Often a dory will ride the curve of a breaking swell while the net setter lets the line move through his gloved hands with resistance enough to keep the stern facing into the sea. If he loses his grip on such a sleigh ride, the boat can broach, broadside, swamp and spill the crew like so much flotsam into the surf.

Before synthetics and before the motorcar, fishermen and dories were limited by the scope of their rowing. Most seining crews worked close to home, leaving a loaded dory high on the beach, rollers at the ready. If the signs were good and the surf negotiable, a crew would likely make a dawn and dusk set, carrying their catch off the beach in horse-drawn wagons. If the fish run was at its peak, crews might make a series of sets, one after the other, along the beach, traveling on foot and in the dory. The hard labor of hand-hauling an ocean seine established its own limits — only so many sets could be made with a seine that could be properly handled only if its length was reasonable. Along Long Island's tempestuous ocean beaches, one hundred to one hundred and fifty fathom (six hundred to nine hundred feet) lengths were maximum for the strongest, most able and most experienced crews. Catches were limited by the tonnages that could be hand carried.

But out of the crucible of global conflict spewed nylon, Dacron, polyethylene and polyurethane. From the carnage at Tobruk came vehicles that could cruise one hundred miles a day over the softest sand. And with these new tools, the haul seiners carved a new image, new procedures, new and limitless techniques. Ocean seines have grown to five hundred fathoms and longer, great haystacks of seines stretching twenty-five to forty feet deep from lead line to cork line. Heaped in the sterns of steel dories nearly thirty

feet long, the seines are no longer set by oarsmen, but spill out in hissing cataracts as outboard motors roar in inboard wells cut where the stern oarsman's seat used to be.

Like rowing and net cleaning, the hauling ritual has been supplanted. Modern haul seiners use two trucks, each with a power winch mounted in back of the cab, to pull both ends of the seine. Pulling lines from the winches are knotted around the twine; in clumsy hands, the engineered horsepower of the winches is enough to rend the net from top to bottom with so little strain on the machines that the winch tender can scarcely feel the rupture.

With more than a half mile of twine heaped in their sterns, plus 100 to 150 fathoms of rope running from the bridles at both seine ends, the dories can spin the web of their nets in arcs that reach more than a quarter mile offshore. The huge seines stretch beyond the outer bar into the very edge of the deep sea, taking a half-circle bite of such dimensions that the total area enclosed is difficult to comprehend.

The sea bottom slopes from the shore to depths of more than thirty feet; the seine becomes a barrier in a water column with an average depth of fifteen feet. If the half-circle bite reaches twelve hundred feet from shore to bunt, and the same distance along the beach, the number of enclosed cubic feet runs beyond the hundreds of millions. A forty-pound striper occupies less than three cubic feet. If a migrating school is packed densely, these new seines can easily circle the entire school.

And they have. Off Cape Hatteras several years ago, a seine was set around one hundred thousand pounds of large bass. More than four thousand fish made up the fifty tons — a single catch so massive that the crew which made the original set sought help from another. As the first crew hauled in its seine, the second made another set just behind the first — catching in the second net the bass that jumped the cork line of the first, or ripped the twine with the sheer weight of their presence in the shallow water.

Just after the war, when men still rowed dories, when they

hauled by hand, or were just learning to use the first, primitive winches and the new, rot-proof synthetic nets, a one-hundred-box haul was the catch of a seiner's dream. At one hundred pounds of fish to a box, ten thousand pounds of stripers was considered the maximum tonnage that any seine and any crew could handle. Stories of hundred-box hauls were part of the regional legend; every crew on the beach could remember every hundred-box haul, and would speak of it reverently, with absolute attention to the details of the time, the crew, the place, and the price eventually paid for the poundage by the brokers at New York's Fulton Fish Market.

Less than twenty years passed before the one-hundred-box legend was shattered by one-thousand-box hauls like the one at Hatteras. Four-hundred- and five-hundred-box hauls quickly became commonplace; seines and the equipment needed to set and retrieve them became devices without limits. Each year, some fisherman added fathoms to last year's net; each year some fisherman developed a system for installing a larger horsepower engine in a larger dory; and each year more powerful trucks groaned onto the beach, their engines roaring with the high revolutions of ever lower gears.

Fishermen in neoprene suits tended their nylon and polyethylene nets, poured fuel into truck tanks, outboard tanks, and the

tanks of the small engines that powered the geared-down winches with their great, slow-turning heads worn polish bright by the sand on ropes pulled wet from the sea across beaches that had known only the grunts of handhauling crews and the whisper of cotton and linen twine for centuries and eons before.

But not even neoprene, nylon and sixty-horsepower outboard motors could take the essential mystery from seining. The sea's secrets are not susceptible to plundering by synthetics or internal combustion engines. Just as Simon Peter was awed by the multitude of fish in his seine after he followed the carpenter's advice, so are today's haul seiners surprised, awed, shocked, dismayed, and sometimes horrified by what their nets retrieve.

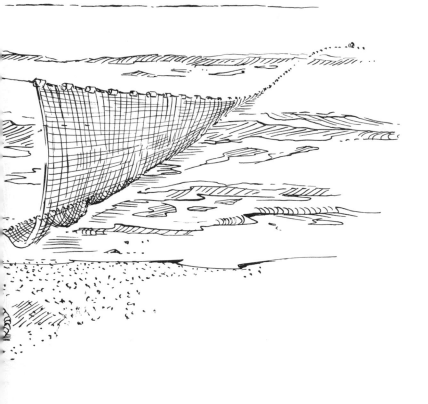

The sea's surface tells the seiners where their nets are, no more. The crescent of floats curves across the Atlantic's rim like a dotted line outlining the teeth of a giant human jaw, but the bite is invisible. The lead line drags across the bottom thirty feet below, stirring muck as it travels its journey of relentless diminution. An angler fish is nudged from the mud by one arm of the seine; across, on the other, a whiptail ray rises from the bottom where it had hidden, flat, dusky and as still as stone. The shrinking arc of the wavering net wall pulls closer; ray and angler meet, their separate and distant worlds now one. The panic of their constraints sends each swimming into the net where the strands bend but seldom break under the strain.

Whatever is inside the seine's arc when the lead line falls is usually found in the twine as the men ashore retrieve their webbing, float following float through the curve of every breaking wave. A thresher shark, twice as long as the tallest man on the crew, rushes the cork line early, sensing danger in the fluttering vibrations of alarm the smaller fish are sending. The shark's scythe tail rises near the float that marks the bunt and is acknowledged by a yell from the men on shore; they are worried that the creature may destroy the seine's center in the muscular contortions of its rage. Some sharks — tigers, hammerheads, whites, blues and makos — know no holding. Once certain of their entrapment, they swim for the surf, turn and charge the net, their enemy. Like a submerged projectile fired from the beach, they hit the twine at express-train speed. The ropes barely shudder as the great fish break clear, rending the net from top to bottom, leaving an open door for the smaller fish who first gave warning.

Often a seine will be set around the sea's own offal: the decaying slime of myriads of dead and dying small jellyfish; the rank mess of rotting vegetation, killed overnight by a swift and silent undersea blight. Or the filth can be the residues of humankind: tar balls from the sluiced holds of crude oil tankers; clustered feces from metropolitan sewers to the west; plastic mementos of a throwaway society — menstrual inserts, condoms, and six-pack rings. Gathered by shoal water crosscurrents, collected by the tides in submerged conglomerations, they are ready to foul the nets and turn the stomachs of seiners who unwittingly surround them with twine.

Like dump pickers, seiners often retrieve civilization's trash. Wings, propellers and twisted bits of the aluminum fuselages of downed aircraft are hauled ashore, sometimes adorned with the remnants of their human purpose: a belt buckle or pen clip. The wreckage of centuries lies in wait for the seiners; ribs of Norse ships rise and fall from their sea-sand graves with the surprise surgings of every storm. On one afternoon, a net will be hauled freely; a single storm later and the lead line will be hung in the protruding ribs of a wooden ship's skeleton. Mines, torpedoes, bombs, casks, oil drums, cans of paint, sonic devices, shell casings and rolls of barbed wire turn up in seines often enough to indicate to anyone wishing to compute the relationship that the entire sea bottom is already contaminated with the castoffs of civilization. During World War II, seiners on Long Island occasionally found in the bunts of their nets the corpses of drowned sailors — some German, some American or Canadian — as if the sea had wearied of becoming a burial ground and had cast the bodies back to the land whence they came.

When the haul goes properly, proper amounts of fish are taken. But even fish can become excessive; the net's bite of the unknown can turn out to be too large to swallow. The seine's arc can cut into a silent, migratory river flowing in thirty feet of water just behind the breakers and, without warning, the seine haulers will find their net straining with the concentrated tonnage of tens of thousands of spiny dogfish, each rubbing its sandpaper hide against the bars of every mesh, each twisting its body so it tangles in the twine, bursting mesh from mesh; and in the immensity of their concentration, splitting the seine itself from cork line to lead line, leaving little or nothing for the fishermen to pull ashore but the wreckage of a design that has triumphed over the centuries.

Instead of washing, weighing, icing, boxing, and labeling a good day's catch, the haul seiners must go over the entire three thousand feet of twine, mending every broken bar, restoring every aspect of the design's integrity. It is a job that can take fishing day after fishing day.

When Simon Peter and his crew followed the carpenter's advice, they "enclosed a great multitude of fishes, and their net brake. . . ." Which is why, perhaps, they left it on the beach and departed with Jesus when he said to them, "Follow me, and I will make you fishers of men."

Haul seining is like that.

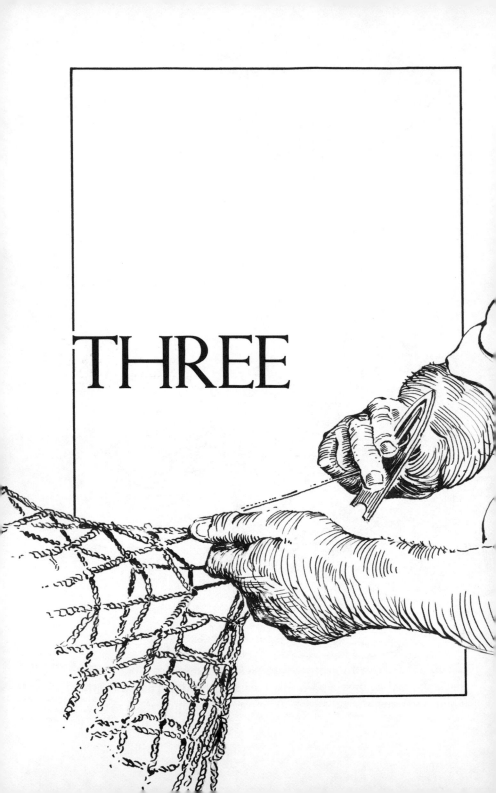

THREE

N ow we are fishing.

A day or so after the Posey crew had passed by while Jim and I painted the *Blue Peril*, Jim changed the plan for spring fishing.

"Why stop with gillnetting?" he asked himself and me as we were loading our new net into our old dory for the first test of the gear. "Why don't we take this twine, add some boughten stuff, put it together around a bunt and we'll have ourselves a seine.

"We'll build a trailer, you can put that Model A on the beach, and we'll have a rig. How about that, Cap? Then we can really catch some fish."

That's how it began — more because Jim and I both wanted to be like the Poseys, even to compete with them, than because we knew what we were getting into or how to go about it. But we began anyway. We made decisions, took steps that allowed us no turning back. Like taking the ferry to Greenport and going to East End Supply to order the netting we needed.

That was a place. A long, wood-frame building near the Greenport docks with a tiny office stuck onto the front, like a bait shack slapped against a barn, the East End headquarters was different from any store I'd been to before. It was more than a store, it was a commercial fisherman's club, his bank, his tool center, meeting place, information source and technical advisor. I had never seen or imagined as much netting as I saw piled on the long floor of the main building. There were dark, tarred herring nets with tiny one-inch meshes; tan netting almost as fine as burlap for whitebait seines; twine with seven- and eight-inch meshes for sturgeon set nets; and all manner of linen and cotton netting for mackerel nets, bluefish runarounds, and haul seines. The twine was stacked everywhere, in bales and mounds that covered the length of the building.

Coils of manila rope filled one corner looking like tree stumps in a forest that had been leveled. Bags of Spanish corks bulged from the loft; and eel pots, chain, clam rakes, bull rakes, anchors, shackles, ring bolts, block and tackles, oars, oarlocks, bailers, bilge pumps, waders, oil coats, boots, knives, boat hooks, gaff hooks, ice picks, life preservers, fire extinguishers, paint, preservative, and seine needles either hung from the rafters, lined shelves, or simply filled empty buckets and galvanized metal garbage cans that were also for sale. Walking through East End Supply I began, for the first time, to understand the scale of the commercial fishing industry.

"These guys don't fool around, do they Jim? I mean, there is a lot of money tied up in this gear. Do you suppose they'll pay any attention to us? All we want is a few hundred feet of netting."

"Don't worry, Cap." Jim turned to one of the East End salesmen. "We're looking for three hundred feet of cotton twine, four-inch mesh, double salvage. Can you help us?"

"How deep do you want it?" The salesman hardly turned around.

"How deep, hmmmm. How deep?" Jim looked up at the rafters, appearing to ponder the question. Jim had a habit of doing that when he didn't want to appear uncertain or confused. It was as if he were designing the seine as he stared into space, but we both knew the twine had to be the same depth as the net we had made that winter. The intensity of his pondering made it look as if he was solving a complex problem, even as he gazed at the ceiling. Then, quickly, as if the solution had come to him in a flash, he turned back to the salesman.

"Twelve feet ought to do it," he said crisply, and that was that.

The salesman pulled 50 fathoms of twine — measuring each six feet with the spread of his outstretched arms — from one of the piles on the floor, cut it and tossed the bundle onto a scale.

"How much would a fellow have to pay for fifty fathoms of twine like that?" Jim asked.

The salesman took the twine off the scale, made a note on his pad and turned to Jim. "About ninety dollars is all."

"We need a bunt to go with it." Jim didn't hesitate a minute about the ninety bucks neither of us had. He went right ahead with his order for the bunt.

"You want us to make that up here?"

"Yep. Send it along as soon as you can. We'll hang this twine in while we're waiting. We'll need corks, leads and rope for that."

The salesman made more notes on his pad. He looked up at Jim. "That's going to run you a total of one hundred and fifty dollars. You fellows from the South Fork, are you?"

Jim said we were, and then explained that we were living with his Uncle Percy, and elaborated on who he was, kept talking, storytelling and name dropping until it appeared the salesman had placed Jim somewhere in his personal reference file. He made a note of Jim's address.

"OK. I'll send along a bill." He looked at us as if he were taking our measurements, reached into one of the buckets near the counter, pulling out a couple of plastic seine needles that had "East End Supply" printed on them. "So you fellows are going to try them, huh. Well, good luck to you. I'll be over that way every now and then, probably run into you."

We said we hoped so, thanked him for the needles and left. I felt like I wanted to run all the way back to the ferry. I couldn't contain myself.

"God damn! We got a net. We just picked it up and walked out. We're going to go seining. We are doing it, Jim. We're really doing it. Jesus Christ, we're doing it."

"Take it easy Cap. Calm down, will you. There's a long way to go yet."

Every morning for the next three weeks, Jim woke me at 5:30. We began work an hour later and kept going until it grew too dark to do any more outdoors. We built a trailer for the dory with oak planks salvaged from the beach, two wheels and an axle we got at a junk yard, a welded steel pipe tongue, held in place by U bolts and fitted with a hitch. We built a roller into the trailer's rear end so we could slide the dory on and off without hurting her tender bottom. We found oversized, bald tires for the Model A and tried her out on the beach with the trailer. We built a net carrier for the seine, also from scrap wood picked up on the beach. We hung in the twine we had bought, attached it and the net we made to either side of the bunt which the salesman had delivered to Percy's. And, in a grand and surprising move, Jim used some of his savings (which he had never touched) to buy a 1924 Reo truck that had been used by the village fire department for years. It was about to be junked when one of Jim's fireman friends told him about it. It was a grand old truck, long and narrow, with a deep bed where firemen had once stood, and its engine made a wonderful roaring noise and moved the Reo along at a fast clip.

Jim loved to drive it through town. "How do you like that, Cap?" he'd yell at me when he whipped through a corner. "Wait till we get a load of bass in here. She'll go just as well with a couple of tons of fish. You'll see."

The entire three weeks we had been getting ready, we had been looking for likely crew members. At least four men would be needed to haul seine properly: one man each on both cork lines, and two more on the lead lines. Two would row, one would set the net and the fourth would stay ashore to hold the inshore end after the set was begun. Five men would make for a full crew; then there would be someone to catch the dory after the set had been made and she came ashore on the back of a wave.

We were ready to go fishing. Everything had been done in three weeks of twelve-hour days, seven days a week, and there were still just the two of us. Experienced fishermen didn't want to take a chance with a green pair like me and Jim. The odd-job men were busy with the spring bustle of a summer resort community; after a lean winter, they had all the work they could handle and were reluctant to give it up for the risky business of seining, and with a small, hand-hauled seine at that.

I kept after Jim, trying to argue him into letting the two of us try it. He wouldn't give in.

"That's no summer ocean there, Cap. You're not back at your place on the dunes, taking a July dip in the surf.

"You've got waders on. The water is cold. And what's going to happen to the net if there's a set running? You think just two of us can hold it against that sort of undertow?"

I had no rebuttal, but I began to wonder if I hadn't been kidding myself ever since the fall. What, after all, had we done? A few sets with the Swede, a winter of wood cutting on other people's land, all that work making the net, the gear, and fixing the Model A. So what the hell had it got us — nothing for me but a bill from East End Supply, of which my share was about ninety bucks. Shit, if we didn't get fishing, what would we do? I didn't want to go back to the city, but I couldn't just hang around the village doing nothing. I began to lie awake nights, kept sleepless by the doubts growling from their cave inside me.

Then Peter turned up.

He had been looking for some sort of fishing job for most of the spring, and even though Jim and I knew him slightly, we hadn't known of his needs, nor he of ours. We discovered each other's in a bar.

I was fooling around with a shuffleboard game, waiting for Jim to finish his set in the three-piece band that he performed with on Fridays and Saturdays. He played the trumpet and tenor sax, changing from one to the other as the tune required, and he took the jobs to keep some money coming in while we waited to get started seining. I envied him. It irritated me to see him blowing; his red, windburned cheeks puffed like two MacIntosh apples and his blue eyes squinting with the strain as he got into the music, got carried away by it, forgot about the fishing and went with the melody. I couldn't play "Chopsticks," couldn't carry a tune, so I fooled around with the shuffleboard game, hoping we'd get a crew and catch so many fish that Jim wouldn't need to play, or would be so tired he wouldn't want to.

Peter just walked up and said hello. That's the way he was — the friendliest man I've ever met.

Peter bubbled like a spring, constantly. It didn't matter what time of the day or night it was, how cold or warm, or how tired, dirty or discouraged Peter might have been — his vitality pushed its way to the top and sparkled there in his smile, his gleaming brown eyes, his friendliness. He was a large man: tall, dark, big across, a dancing bear. He seemed always on the point of embrace, about to sweep me into the bear hug of his long arms, to breathe his smile into my face. For him, it wasn't enough that he could laugh through any situation, he wanted us to join the laughter, to participate in his vitality, to share the energies that coursed through him like bright water burbling from a rock.

He came from a house on the dunes just two houses west of my boyhood's white chimneys. I had indeed known him most of my life in the sense that he had been a presence in each of my summers. He sailed, fooled around the ocean's edge, had occasional parties at his house. We tended to visit each other mainly in the early and late weeks of the season, before and after the summer's central months. That was because his family was not a social family, although they were quite proper, accepted by everyone, and claimed as friends by many who hardly knew them.

But Peter's parents, his several aunts and uncles and his numerous cousins seldom acknowledged what my parents considered social necessities. His clan lived totally around that large, outermost house on the dunes, finding sustenance in their shared enthusiasms. They sailed races against each other on the lake in a collection of wonderfully disparate craft; they had nightly picnics on the beach with driftwood fires that lit up the sky and became a kind of beacon for me, leading me away from the structured summers of tennis lessons and club lunches. There was, in that shingled, arching house that rose like yet another dune from the line of dunes it occupied, a sweep of summer excitement so constant and so electric that each time I went through the sun-bleached, unpainted doors I felt as if I had crossed an ocean and stepped ashore in a new summer land altogether different from the one I inhabited at the house with the white chimneys less than a mile to the east.

I never knew what most of Peter's relatives worked at, or what their professions might be. In the summer they kept the house filled with magazines and papers and books I never saw elsewhere; they did watercolor paintings of birds, caught and mounted butterflies, kept fish in large saltwater aquariums, and spent most of their time outdoors when the weather was decent. I remember that Peter's Uncle Will once showed me a school of spearing in the warm shallows at the edge of the lake. He hit the water hard with the heel of his hand, splashing some of the silversides on the beach, picked one up in his fingers and bit off most of it, tossing the head back into the lake.

"How tasty," he said. "The Japanese eat raw fish. We should learn more about that."

When Peter walked up to me at the shuffleboard table it was difficult for me to connect him with his Uncle Will, that wonderfully eccentric summer family and the winged gray house on the dunes. This was not Peter's season, yet here he was, smiling and reaching out for me, giving me his big bear hug.

"Peter, what are you doing here?"

"I'm here, that's what. I'm living here, in the Springs. I got married last winter and now we live here year 'round. The house was torn down, you know, sold to someone from the city. But I got the sun porch, had it moved all the way to the Springs and made a home out of it."

That sun porch. I could still see it, looming at the west end of the house on the dunes like an oversize fan-tail on a gray galleon, its walls mostly small, rectangular glass panes each stitched in place with thin threads of sash. We would sit in there with a fire going on stormy days and watch salt spume from the ocean waves blow across the sand onto the sun porch windows.

"But Peter, what are you doing? Do you have a regular job?"

"No, not really. This and that, this and that."

I waited until the band had finished its set and went over to talk with Jim.

"See that guy over there. That's Peter. He's not doing much. How about him for the crew?" I didn't know if Jim and Peter had met before. Jim said they had, just once or twice, but Jim liked Peter's size, the physical presence that spoke so of strength.

When Jim asked him if he wanted to try haul seining with us, Peter said, "Sure," in such a confident way, with a broad and beaming smile.

His endless energy and the nudging of his smile got us going. Jim went back to see Alex, a man who had already turned us down, and persuaded him to give the crew a try. Alex worked as a gardener for one of the village's largest estates, but the place he tended was occupied only during July and August, so he could fish with us in the early morning and again in the late afternoon. And with Alex's help, we enlisted Bumps, a village policeman who worked the night shift. He said he could meet us after he got off at four in the morning, fish for a while, go home for a sleep and meet us again in the late afternoon.

Jim, Peter, Alex, Bumps and me — that was the crew. None of us had ever hauled seine before, but Alex was a fine mechanic, strong and unafraid. Bumps was a good cop, a community policeman with a sense of humor and not so much to do on the night shift in the quiet town that he would show up weary for fishing. Besides, he was stocky enough and bright eyed enough to rival Peter in general enthusiasm.

So, now we are fishing.

We make our first set — the first of my life, and of Jim's, Peter's, Alex's and Bumps's — early on the morning of a day in the third week of May. It is midseason; we hear the Poseys have caught stripers already — boxes of them. That thought helps pump our adrenalin to even more thumping levels as the Model A turns off the road onto the Coast Guard beach about a half hour before sunup.

The trailer is in tow, the *Blue Peril* is on the trailer and the new seine is loaded in her stern. Peter, Bumps and Alex ride in the back of the "A" — converted since wood cutting to a jerry-built, pickup truck configuration. Jim drives and I sit with him in the cab — still unrepaired from scars it suffered under the falling oak. I am amazed the car can carry such a load and still pull the trailer. Each of us knows the load is severe, too much really, which is why we come down the bluff off the tar road and go straight across the beach to begin our set. We don't want to give the car a chance to break down before we make this first haul.

The wind is soft, southeast. Light air. The sea is almost a summer sea, glassy, the waves shimmering at their curling centers, their sound made softer by the gentleness of the May warmth already in the air. Terns dip like dandelion seeds to the sea's surface, then up, following the whim of the wind. They are summer birds, and give me a summer feeling as I watch them feathering across the rising sun's first morning mark, orange on the water.

Jim backs the trailer down to the sloping sand at the white water's edge. The rest of us slide the dory off; she goes easily on the roller. Jim is pleased with his work.

"Just like New York," he says as he drives the "A" higher on the beach and comes to join us. Peter will row amidships; I am

on the bow oars. I can feel the pressure and the coolness of the sea pressing against the feet of my waders as I stand in the wash holding the dory in place. My heart is pounding. The dory heaves slightly as the wash rolls under her. It seems to me that Jim waits a long, long time. Then he says it.

"Get in, John.

"Get in, Peter.

"Pull!"

We are rowing the *Peril* in the open Atlantic as Jim sets the seine. We make a passable set, reaching the back of the breakers just as the jack and the last of the net go over. Jim holds us there, looking out to sea, past the bar, waiting for a slatch.

"Go," he yells, and we are ashore where Bumps waits to grab the dory's bow as she slides onto the sand.

When we get up on the beach and see the smallness of the arc our cork line makes in relation to the vastness of the ocean, we realize that ours is a small net indeed. Still, it takes a good half-hour to haul it in, hand over hand. I am on the cork line at one end, working with Alex who is on the lead line. I have learned something already: after rowing and pulling the dory to high ground, the walk to the other end of the net seems like a long one, and my waders get heavier with each step.

Jim had put four corks on one line and painted them white, then tied the line to the top of the bunt to mark the center of our seine. Ever since we started hauling, I have been watching the white corks move closer. Now, the marker is just in back of the breakers and I know it is only a matter of minutes before the bunt will be ashore and will discover what we have caught.

There is a flash in the wash — a movement in the shallow white water. I am not certain of what I am seeing, but it is there, again. A lateral movement, a presence that is not part of the wave but is still so much part of the sea that it is difficult to discern.

As the net moves still closer, the flash becomes a pale fin, cutting the white water for a second.

I hear myself yelling. "There's a fish there. See, there. I can feel it thumping." And I can. The cork line strums in my hand, softly, like the beat of a distant drum, like my pounding heart.

The bunt is in the waves now. We see the striper in the wash. It turns seaward, flips its tail and rockets into the cod end — the very end of the purse that is the bunt. It is our first, and, for this set, our only bass. There are sand dabs, several skates and some alewives in the cod end. Jim unties the slip knot, the bass slides out onto the beach and Jim picks it up by the gills and heaves it higher on the sand. It lies there, its tail slapping. Jim walks up, nudges it with one toe of his waders and says, "We're going to see more of you."

We clean the crabs out of the net, put the dory on the trailer and load the wet net in her stern. Our first bass goes into the back of the "A" and we are ready to make a second set.

Our beginning sets a pattern. The May weather holds. Still, gentle mornings become bright, splendid days, full of sun and afternoon breezes from the southwest. For nine days, we make at least one set a day, and sometimes as many as four. But there are only two four-set days. We discover early how much of a strain gear must take to fish from the beach. The Model A is our weakest link. She boils over, gets stuck, and sometimes stalls out, refusing to restart, like a tired, stubborn mule that won't move until it gets its proper rest.

The trailer hitch bends under the weight of the dory, heavier now that she has soaked in some sea water, and carries a wet, sandy net loaded off the beach instead of dry and clean from Jim's yard. A tire leaks; on one set we haul through a caravan of spider crabs, on the move, unseen, scuttling in quiet regiments toward an engagement we will never witness. We find most of their thousands tangled in our twine and spend the rest of the day picking them from the meshes, carefully, so their spiked shells and small, raspy claws don't fray the cotton.

It is discouraging. One afternoon Alex does not show up and the four of us set without him. The southwest wind has got a set going to the east; choppy waves break at an angle to the beach and the entire inshore ocean flows east like a river. In the spring the sets are made from east to west; in theory, the stripers are moving east and the seine is dropped in front of them. Rowing against the chop is difficult; rhythm cannot be maintained, the dory is slapped around, won't glide as she should. But hauling in the seine is worse.

Tugged by the waves' lateral slide, the seine deforms. Instead of a half-circle that shrinks in size but maintains the integrity of its arc as it is hauled ashore, the net caught in the southwest set flattens along its western wing and bulges at the east. With the down-beach current moving at nearly five miles an hour, Jim and Peter can hardly walk fast enough in their waders to keep the twine coming ashore. The sea is powering it away from them in a physics for which we have no response. While the lines hum with tension at the west end, Bumps and I strain to retrieve the bulge slack fast enough. We can not. Gradually our end angles off to the east so that the arc is now a steep angle, both sides straight, with the bunt being forced inshore and the two wings of the net surging toward each other until they meet and tangle in fruitless and fishless confusion.

It is all we can do to keep the sea from wrenching our net from us. It's as if the Atlantic is trying to take the cotton, corks, leads, and manila that robs her of her creatures, and leave us stripped of the primary tool of our daily invasion of her territory. When we do get the seine ashore, we are exhausted. We sit there on the damp sand, contemplating the single line of distorted twine the net has become, and we wonder how we shall find the strength to put it back in order and to load it once again into the dory.

We do, and even as we load the last few fathoms, the wind drops off as the sun sets. Jim looks at the red sun rolling over the dunes behind us. "Looks good for tomorrow morning. Alex or no Alex, we're going to give it another try."

Jim is right about the weather. Gentled by a windless night, the surf is relatively stable when we arrive the next dawn, easing the "A" through the same tracks we left the evening before — almost the same tracks we made that morning when we set the seine for the first time here on the Coast Guard beach.

Alex is not with us, and neither is the excitement of three weeks ago. The softness of late May and early June has sapped us with its persistence; each dawn has given us fishing weather; there have been no full days when we could rest with the legitimate relaxation a storm could bring. Our weariness is emotional as well as physical. Just as we can not leap from the beach to the trailer, neither can we hear our hearts pounding with anticipation as we hold the *Blue Peril* in the wash waiting for Jim to give us the word to row. When he says, "Get in, John," this morning, though, he tries to cut our fatigue with a feathering of humor. He spreads out my name in a nasal exaggeration of the East End accent. It comes out, "Jaawn," and makes us smile.

Jim is so persistent, so stubborn, so steady, so unforgiving. I watch him as I row through the set, reaching, heaving, reaching. Pausing, slowing, studying the bunt to make certain it is properly positioned, then heaving, reaching again as we move on. Peter bubbles behind me on the bow oars.

"By Jesus," Jim says, "you better be setting around some fish. I'm going to have to boil up these waders for my supper if we don't get something besides a dry haul soon."

"Come on, Jaawn," Peter laughs, picking up Jim's foolishness, "pull before them bass escape."

When we're ashore I jog east along the beach to join Bumps and begin hauling. The new sun is in my eyes; it strokes a listless sea and, as I have each morning for the past week, I wonder what the hell we do this for, day after day. Bumps surprises me.

"Get on this lead line John, and keep it down. I could swear I feel some fish bumping in there."

"That's wishful thinking Bumps, that's what that is." But I feel a tremor pulse in me like an electric charge. The hauling is easier. Unlike me, who sees fish in every set, Bumps has never said anything like this before. I hear a yell from the other end. It's Peter, his voice slicing the distance like a loon's call.

"Look at that! Look at that!"

I can see the silhouette of a gilled bass hanging from the twine at Peter's end. Sometimes that means a bunch of fish are in the net — enough so that some have panicked and rushed the twine. Other times, it is a false sign, meaning only that one fish has somehow erred. Still, I pull even more diligently, more carefully. And my heart pounds.

But none of us is ready for the explosion that begins when we start hauling the quarters (the sections of stronger twine on each side of the bunt).

As the quarters begin to show in the waves, inching straight through the curving crests, the white-water wash inside the net's shrinking V begins to tremble as if an earthquake is shaking it from beneath the sand. As the first of the quarter twine comes heavily into my hand, the wash is suddenly gone, replaced by the thrashing bodies of more striped bass than I have ever seen before. And they are huge — bulls and cows, most of them over thirty pounds.

They roll, they run, their broad tails slap at the sand. There is so much concentrated movement in this single watery space directly before us that it is without order and pattern. It is a living explosion, prolonged beyond any believing — an energy release of such intensity that we are awed, silent for a moment in the presence of these creatures and their struggle for escape, for life. The wet sounds are everywhere, the foam flies and the fish race toward the beach, turn and propel themselves back to the sea — silver and bronze projectiles aimed at the places where the lead line is lifted by ridges in the sand, or by our own inattention as we stand there, battered by the reality of our dreams come to life.

The four of us begin screaming. There may be an attempt at instruction in the screams, but the cries are primarily released tension, awe, excitement and a sudden terror that in the abyss of our own inexperience we shall lose the entire haul.

But the new twine is strong, the bunt capable of expanding far beyond its appearance. As we hold the lead lines and the corks up, the bass pack and gather in the bunt's long purse until we have a stretched net sack of huge fish that wallows back and forth like a bag packed full of massive, long, flexible pearls.

It is then we realize that the net holds more than we can move onto the land — more than a ton of fish. Four of us can not haul them by hand up the sloping angle of the beach. Denied their freedom to swim, the bass become a burden, and we pull on the net as we might if we had set around one of Egypt's pyramids and tried to pull it across the desert. We can not budge the bunt.

"Hold on, hold on," Jim yells at Peter, and hands him the twine on their wing, both lead line and cork line. Jim runs for the "A," wraps a rope around the front bumper, runs to the surf and takes several hitches with the rope's other end around the bunched twine near the bunt. Then back he runs to the "A," starts her up and uses the old car to pull. With the three of us heaving and grunting and the "A" snorting and slipping her clutch, the laden bunt moves another ten feet. That is as far as the entire combination of our physical and mechanical capacities can take it.

"What's the tide doing?" Jim yells, then answers his own question. "It's falling. If we can just hold them here awhile, we'll have room to work."

So we wait. The bunt rests ponderously in the surf, its stretched meshes cutting into the bellies of several stripers. The rope to the Model A stays taut; we keep pressure on the lines. We sit there stupidly on the sand, panting and grunting, staring at the huge, dying bass, and bewildered at the scope of our slaughter, wondering if we will be lucky enough to harvest the creatures we have killed.

We are saved by the falling tide. As the sea drops away from us, tugged from this stretch of beach by a moon on the other side of the planet, we can stand in the wash, untie the line that closes the bunt's ringed cod end and make an opening just large enough so that while Jim holds the opening high to keep the fish from wriggling free, we can reach in, grab a big bass through its gill slit, tug it from the twine and carry it clumsily up the beach, above the water line where we drop it onto a pile and go back for another.

After twenty minutes of this, the three of us have taken out enough fish so that we can tug the bunt to higher ground. We have spent two hours on the beach; the sun is high now, growing warmer. The bass are drying in the heat, their scales stiffening with sand. We load the "A" full with the fish, heaving them like logs. It takes two trips to get the fish to Jim's yard, then another to pick up the dory and the net. It is noon before we get off the beach; we have been working since 4:30 in the morning. We are shaking with fatigue and excitment; no one has thought to ponder the possible reward for the work. We are too proud about our success as seiners.

By three in the afternoon, after Jim has made a run to Ted's packing plant for fish boxes, we have washed, weighed, iced and boxed the bass for shipment that evening to Fulton Market. We have a total of twenty-three boxes — a bit more than 2300 pounds of fish. We load the boxes in the Reo to take them to Ted's where the New York truck will stop. It is after five when we leave Ted's. We have not eaten since morning, and I'm sitting there in the truck in my waders thinking only about the money we may get if the price holds at twenty cents a pound. Shared up five ways, the haul could earn us almost a hundred bucks apiece.

I babble to Jim about my arithmetic all the way from Ted's to his mother's kitchen table.

I'm still babbling the next morning. Dressing in the dark I feel a kind of manic pressure to get back to the beach. I want another haul like yesterday's.

Alex has heard of our luck, and he shows up, even though he knows he won't get a share of the haul he missed. That's how it works. But he is as eager as I am.

"Back her down, Jim," he says when we get to the Coast Guard beach. "Back her down."

Jim does. The *Peril,* still on the trailer, is poised at the ocean's edge, but Jim dosen't tell us to roll her off. He is standing there, looking offshore. He points to a curving swell.

"See that, Cap. That looks good size to me. Sharp, too." The wave, just after those words, collapses with a hollow boom, a kind of captive thunder that begins within the tunnel of the steep-sided sea. Something has changed during the night as I dreamed of another haul. Some elemental tremor has shaken the sea floor hundreds of miles from here, sending a surge of swells to surface on a windless sea and roll silently to distant shores where, at last, the thunder born in an undersea canyon resounds against the land.

I am shattered by the doubt in Jim's voice. "Christ, Jim, we can get off. Come on. We've got to go. God damn, think of the fish that could be here."

I start tugging at the *Peril* trying to nudge her off the trailer. Peter and Bumps look at Jim. Alex gets on the dory's other side and gives me a hand. For a long spell, Jim doesn't move, doesn't say anything. Then he makes his decision.

"OK, but if we're going we'd better go now. Those seas look as if they're growing, not easing off."

I hold hard to the dory's gunwales in the wash, frantic with the wish for just one more good haul, another twenty boxes, but trembling with the ground beneath me each time a breaking swell thunders on the shore.

Peter looks down the beach. "Here come the Poseys." He points to a truck in the distance — a dot on the white line of the sand. "They must have heard about our catch. Let's go, before they get here."

With Bumps and Alex pushing through up to their waists in the wash, we make it off the beach — just. I can see alarm in Jim's eyes as he watches one of the swells close in on us. But Peter and I pull hard enough to get us over the crest. We slap down hard on the other side, but we are behind the breaking seas. How eerie it is on this warm, windless morning to feel the dory rise and fall so steeply. I am relieved when the set is done, the jack goes overboard and we wait for a slatch that will give us a chance to get ashore.

We wait, and we wait. Five minutes, ten minutes. Each of us can tell the swells are growing. We hear a slight hissing offshore, like the whisper of dry leaves blowing along Main Street in the fall. One of the swells has crested on the outer bar, its top wavering like a lace fringe in a breeze. The crest does not topple, there is no white water, just that wavering, hissing bit of lacework at the top.

"See that!" says Peter. "Did you see that? We better get ashore."

Jim waits until the swell has moved beneath us and thundered on the beach where Bumps is waiting. Then he yells "Go," and Peter and I row hard. The ash oars bend, the empty *Peril* scoots for the sand.

We are not quick enough. A second, shadow swell is behind the large one. We find ourselves surfing on its forward curve, too fast. Jim can not hold the seine rope tightly enough to keep our stern seaward. We broach, swing side-to, and the swell rolls the *Peril* over, dumping us into the wash. Jim jumps clear at the stern, but Peter and I are under the overturned dory, churning, bumping and sliding in our watery, dark, turbulent and airless prison.

I know I should escape, but I can not know how, or in what

direction. I do not panic, I do not think. I am merely there, weight-less in the dark water, sensing only the most distant of instinctive messages that I could be drowning.

Hands grapple for me, clutch at my waders, my oil coat, then yank me from under the dory and pull me toward the surface. Once I can see light and get a sense of up and down, I push to my feet. My head and shoulders rise clear of the wash. I am standing in the surf and as the brine leaves my eyes I can see that it is Ted who has hauled me from the sea. Just in front of me I see Peter with Ding standing beside him. Ding's rawboned face is wet, he is laughing and yelling.

"Got ya, didn't it. Shit, that was something. Rolled her right over, it did. Now look at me. Soaked. What the hell am I going to tell the old lady when I walk in with these wet clothes?"

Ted leans toward me, yells in my ear over the surf's roaring. "You OK, boy? You want to be careful on them sharp seas."

"Yes, I'm OK." Ted is walking back to the beach, slowly and awkwardly in waders that are half-full of salt water. He and Ding go to the big, silver truck and take off the waders, dump out the water, put the waders on again and, with the rest of the Posey crew, give us a hand hauling the seine.

The winches on the Posey trucks make the work so easy that the set is done before I have much of a chance to think about what might have happened. A half-dozen small bass are in the bunt.

Ted walks over to look at them. "Well, that's a few anyway. Enough to pay for your gas.

"I guess you had most of your luck yesterday. It isn't too often you get luck two days running. Can't push too hard, don't you know. Got to work with the sea, not against it. Can't beat it, no matter how you try."

I'm standing there with him by the bunt, my soaked clothes weighting me down. I feel stupid, numb, let down. Jim opens the bunt, dumps out the fish, looks at me.

"How do you like it now, Cap?"

I can't answer.

Smiley calls from the silver truck, standing there in that same long, black overcoat. I have to grin.

"Come on, Ted, come on," he says. "We ain't going to set today, no sir, no sir, not with them seas. I want to get home and pick some strawberries. Makes me horny, them berries do."

Ted laughs. He's helping me hank out the seine, getting it ready to load in the dory.

"That's OK, Ted. Thanks, I can handle it."

"We help each other, don't we, Johnny? That's how we get along on this beach, ain't it? Got to help each other."

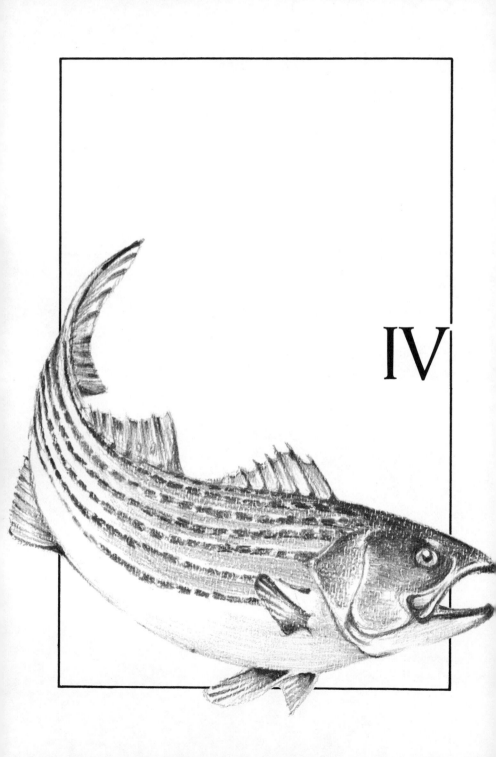

IV

The plover begin gathering in August. Small flocks of goldens and black-bellieds stand near each other at the ends of sand bars, or cluster on the mud flats at low tide. When clammers approach, the birds take wing, circling, and the crystal whistle of their calls echoes across the marsh — a pure and lonely sound that is autumn's earliest prelude.

Plover have a distance to travel; the goldens will fly some 2,500 miles from eastern Long Island to their South American wintering grounds on the pampas. Perhaps that is why they are the first to gather, and why their restless flights from point to marsh to mud-flat are a signal that sets every other creature to fluttering, flashing and twitching at the silent calling of the season.

Movement begins as the equinox approaches in late September. Line storms roll up the coast from Hatteras, anointing the East End with a warm and tropical wetness, with southeast winds, fat, splattering raindrops and great gouts of fog that slide over the island like a cloth over a table.

The weathercock turns overnight; in the morning the wind is northwest — electric in its dryness, vital in its chill. It is a wind for journeys. The plover leave, propelled by the clarity of the moment, nudged south by the nor'wester at their backs. Their places on the points and in the marshes are taken by yellowlegs, next to follow in the plover's course. Hawks move down from Canada and Maine, carving the sky with the swords of their flight, swooping on starlings, redwings, cowbirds and swallows who imitate the plover, bunching in flocks along telephone wires in dotted semaphores that signal to the high falcons.

Even as the birds sweep aloft, fish twitch beneath the sea, finding in their shared migratory compulsion a common thread that crosses eons as it traverses the entire evolutionary tapestry until it reaches a time when there was only sea, and all the creatures of the sky were still submerged. Just as the plover ride the wind more than two thousand miles, so do blowfish, herring, menhaden, fluke, flounder, bluefish, and striped bass ride the invisible currents of the Atlantic to wintering places, some yet unknown and undiscovered.

It is the gathering of the fish that prompts the most wonder. No flock of plover, no massive formation of high flying geese could approach the scale of the schools of bass and bluefish that gather off Montauk Point every October in readiness for the autumnal journeys that mimic the flights overhead.

From the gunk holes of Gardiners Island, the sand flats of Napeague, the rocks of Cuttyhunk, the gullies of the Race, the rips of Plum Gut, and the surf from Seguin to Shinnecock — from every inshore location of the North Atlantic from Maine's St. John River to the furthest reaches of Long Island Sound, striped bass and bluefish move and gather and school. The mass of their collected numbers covers acres of sea surface and the turmoil of their traveling thrashes the water white with foam that ripples like tall grass in the wind.

What could the sight have been like before the boats came? What was the scale of these migrations before Capt. John Smith sailed the same coast? Did the Mohawk and the Montauk take their canoes into the bays and open sea to witness the turmoil more closely, or were they so awed by the scope of the schooling that they kept to their beaches, fearful that the fish might swamp the Indian craft in the frenzy of their flailing? Even with the sound of one hundred propellers turning, with the waters crisscrossed by one hundred fishing boats, the surfacing of bass and bluefish is breathtaking to behold.

When the sea was unscarred by any wake, when no single sailing ship hissed through the schools, the schools of fish must have been monumental. Their journey must have set the water to dancing for miles; a ribbon of life must have run from Peconic to the Point, tying the ocean and the sound together with a band of silver.

The energy inherent in such masses adds to the excitement of the season — an excitement so compelling that it must stem from the same ageless threads, instinctual strands that link humankind with bird and fish. Like the plover in flight, men's spirits soar in the Yankee autumn. Like the fish flashing on the surface, men move through the nor'west wind with greater speed, greater purpose, greater verve now than at any other time of the year.

As the wind pushes at Orient and Montauk from the northwest, it rides across the sound, coming from the White Mountains and beyond, bringing Canada's coolness, cumulus and clarity. The wind spills apples in its path, it fills lungs with purpose, sets pulses racing, forbids sleep past dawn. Watch any door open on a nor'west October morning in any eastern, Atlantic community, and you watch men and women set forth with magnificent confidence and jauntiness to their steps. There are no longer any questions about life's design; the wind sweeps doubt away as quickly as it dispels the equinoctial fogs. Painters paint, writers write, farmers harvest, storekeepers smile, carpenters build, sailors cast off, and fishermen fish.

They do it with a zest unknown at any other time, through the blue days of October and on into November, sustained so by the season that the month's grayness goes almost unnoticed, so sturdy is the autumnal exhilaration. Those humans who go to sea, who witness the migratory massing of the striped bass and the bluefish even as they also witness the flocking of the black ducks, the wavering lines of southbound scoters, and the lofty movements of the Canada geese, these are the humans who are propelled into an extra dimension of activity. So contagious is the excitement, so shared the cascade of released energy that fishermen find themselves going without sleep, missing meals, lifting loads, hauling nets, navigating boats, making plans and dreaming dreams that are as golden as the turning leaves on a sugar maple, as dramatic as the pheasant in full plumage, full flight.

It is as if the writhing rivers of moving fish, pulsing through the Atlantic's submerged arteries, also set the fishermen's blood to coursing with the same elemental energy. The air intoxicates, the tumultuous sea generates hallucinations of immortality so convincing that every fisherman charges through October as if winter never waited on the other side, as if there were no end to the migrations, as if the great schools of stripers were part of an endless river flowing from some boundless source — a resource without limits, a season without sadness, a time without end.

That is the magic that rides on the striper's shoulders as it swims through the ageless pattern of its autumnal migration, south along the shore and deep into the souls of the men who live on it.

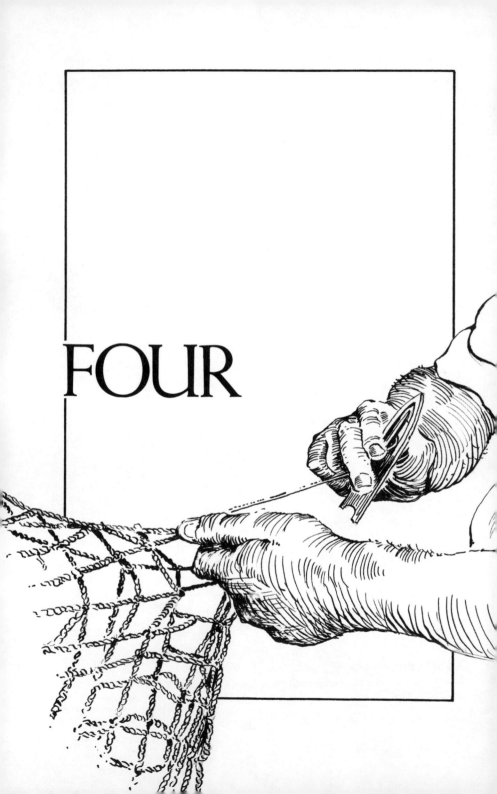

FOUR

A breeze from the northwest feathers my cheeks as I walk from the Model A to Ted's back door. He is up. I can tell because the bare-bulb light over the door shines blindingly in the predawn darkness, casts long shadows over the dooryard where Ted's big silver truck is parked, complete with a seine-heavy dory on the attached trailer.

I wait there in the light, at the bottom of the cement steps with their steel-pipe railing. No one has told me, but I would bet that Ted built the forms, poured the cement and made the railing — probably traded a fish or two for the pipe. I wait for Jim to clamber out of the "A." He takes his own sweet time, checking to make certain he has his gloves, his oil coat, his wool-knit pullover cap, and his brown banana for breakfast.

He walks out of the dark in his waders, a black shape waddling into the circle of light, moving quietly across the decades of crushed clam and scallop shells that make a parking lot of Ted's front yard. He stops and looks at the stars, hard and bright in the cloudless sky. He points up at them. "Nice morning, Cap. They don't come better in October."

As far as I'm concerned, they don't come any better any time of the year. It is all I can do to sleep through the short nights that we have left when we leave Ted's at six or seven in the evening. We have to be back at four every morning, and sometimes, when we get fish on the "sunset" haul of the day before, we don't get home until nine or ten. Five hours sleep seems to be enough for me; it has been ever since we joined Ted's crew.

We saw him and Ding and Smiley and the rest of the spring crew quite often after that morning he pulled me from under the *Peril*. The summer came and Jim and Peter and I quit seining. Peter and I spent the summer digging clams, and in the early fall we went scalloping, waiting for the bass to begin their migration. Jim was still on his summer job as a mate on one of the charter boats at the Montauk Yacht Club. Between us, we'd agreed to begin bassing about the first of October.

But before that, we got a phone call from Ted.

"Want to give the bass a try?" That was the first thing he said. I wasn't sure I understood.

"Well I'll tell you, Johnny, Ding and Lindy got their own rig this season. They're leaving me with Smiley, that's all. I thought you and Jim and Peter could come with me. Bring that Model A, we'll get a winch with a Briggs and Stratton for her. She'll do OK if she don't have to pull a dory. You'll get a quarter-share for the car, plus a share for each of you. I always treat my crews fair. You ask anybody about that."

It wouldn't have made any difference to me if I'd been told I wouldn't get any sort of a share. The idea of fishing with Ted, one of the best of the Poseys — who were the best of the fishermen — was enough to set me to yelping with glee. That huge truck, that long seine, those powerful winches, the equipment and skills that had been acquired over four generations of fishermen — I was going to get in on all this after just a year on the East End. I could hardly believe my luck.

Like me, Peter was all smiles. He was most of the time anyway, but the notion of fishing with Ted gave him a prospect he rolled over in his fancies during the entire last week we were clamming. He'd stand there in the bow of the *Emma*, yanking at the handle of his bull rake, grunting with each pull, fashioning a running monologue on the days we were soon to see.

"Jawn, when we get started with — grunt — Ted, we're just as likely to get — grunt — a hundred-box haul as we are to get ten — grunt. Good Gawd, Johnny, what are we going to do — grunt — with all that money?"

"I'll tell you, John, what I'm going to do. I'm going to — grunt — get me a set of waders that don't leak, and — grunt — I'm going to throw this bull rake so far out in the bay no one will ever be able to find it. Not even me — grunt — if I'm ever stupid enough to think I want to go clamming again."

But Jim wasn't so sure joining up with Ted would be a good thing. "Why do you think he called us, John? Did you ever puzzle over that? Here we are, three guys who've only been on the beach for one season. We might as well be men off the street as far as our experience is concerned. But Ted calls us.

"Well, he does know us, knows who we are. Maybe he thinks you're rich, Johnny, coming from that big house on the dunes. Maybe he wants you to finance a new rig. Ha, wouldn't that be a laugh!"

Jim grabbed me by the arm. "That's what did it, Cap. Not your money, your muscles." He squeezed my biceps — a meager lump at best. "Wiry, that's what you are, Cap," he laughed. "Like a steel cable, them arms are." He broke up at his joke.

"No, Ted needs us, that's why he called. He needs the Model A. He needs some young studs who are crazy enough about fishing to get up at three or four every morning, work in the cold and wet all day, row that great ark of a dory of his against the chop, get covered with sand and fish gunk, not eat any lunch, and haul seine all day, some days for nothing more than a couple of sand dabs and sea robins. Probably average out we'll make something like fifty cents an hour for working twelve-hour days, seven days a week. Now what do we get out of that, Cap? What do we get out of that?"

I'd been thinking a good deal about what I was getting out of fishing, but my thoughts would not have given Jim the answer he was looking for. He was half joking; he wanted some reply like, "A busted back and a flat billfold," but I had been thinking about what I had learned, about the people I had met, about how good I felt when I got a word of praise from Jim on my rowing, or when I looked at three full bushels of clams after a day's digging and realized that I had done that work quite on my own, out on a bay one hundred miles from New York City — a bay that tens of thousands of people looked at every month without ever seeing more than the reflection of the sky on its surface, if they even saw that. I knew what I was getting out of fishing, even though I didn't understand some of the reasons for my total involvement with an occupation that had been alien to me for all but one year of my life.

I was getting a kind of companionship, a fellowship, a friendship I had never known before except with my two brothers. I was getting outdoor physical activity that was putting muscles on my thin frame, in spite of Jim's joshing. I was working long hours, but they were hours totally free, free of the hierarchical, rank-happy system I had found in the Army Air Force, and free of the subservience that had been an inevitable part of the public relations job in the city. And most of all I was getting a rush of enthusiasm such as I had never known, or even visualized. Nothing in my total experience had prepared me for the excitement I found in fishing day after day with no letup in my thumping adrenalin level, no matter how much one day was like another, how small the catch, or how seemingly pointless the hours of waiting on the beach for a school of striped bass to show on the surface.

That's what I was getting out of it, but I said to Jim, "I don't know, Cap. I guess we'll get a busted back and a flat billfold. But we'll do the same on our own, so why not try it with Ted? At least he's got winches. We won't lose any more hauls because we can't hold the net when a set is running."

"OK Cap," Jim said, "I'll give it a try, for this one season." I was surprised at this limitation, but I knew Jim meant what he said. I began to understand just how much he wanted to become his own fisherman, to become better than the Poseys. For him, fishing had no mysteries. As Jim saw it, if he worked hard enough, long enough and smart enough, he could decipher the sea.

As we stand under the light, waiting for Ted to come to the door, Jim looks at his brown banana. "Finest kind," he says, "finest kind."

When we're inside, Ted pours us each a cup of instant coffee, tosses a piece of toast to each place at the oilcloth-covered kitchen table. We're free to spread the toast with peanut butter from the jar in the table's center. This is Ted's home kitchen, and he has given us breakfast each morning for the week we have been fishing with him. It's the same breakfast every time, and it's nothing special; but there aren't many other skippers who would do as much.

Ted looks at me as I munch my toast. "You have beefsteak last night for supper, did you Johnny? I can tell you did. The blood is in your cheeks. Nothing like beefsteak to make you horny, is there? Come on now, Johnny, tell me. Did you have some?"

Now there is blood in my cheeks. "Yes Ted, I did. But I don't believe it makes me look any different."

"Course it does. Course it does." He looks at the door. "There's Peter, coming now. I wonder what happened to that damn Smiley. Good weather like this, we want to be out early. Get that first set in before sunup, before those bass even know we're on the beach."

Peter comes through the door, large and loud. "We're going to get them today. Oh yes, we are. I can feel it, Cap. I just know it. Aren't I right, Ted?"

"They can be there any day. They are there, every day. We just have to find them, is all. Can get a hundred boxes just as easy as one. As long as we set that twine around fish, we can catch five tons . . . or ten tons, if we want." Ted gets up from his chair, pulling up the suspenders on his waders. "But we can't catch bass here in the kitchen. That twine's got to be in the water. Now if Smiley was here, we could leave. Isn't it something. He lives closest, but you fellows are all here before him."

We move outdoors, in single file through the door — four bulky, black figures in our chest-high, big-footed waders — and walk over to the narrow tar road that runs through Poseyville. It's called Poseyville because, on· this stretch of cross highway about two city blocks long, the entire Posey clan has its homes, its fishing shacks, its boats, its gear, its families, its vegetable gardens and the leavings of a century of fishing the waters of the East End.

Set between East Hampton and Amagansett, two of the Island's wealthiest villages, Poseyville looks like a landscape that drifted in from the sea, or was left in the wake of a tidal wave that washed over the land. It looks as if it should have been cleaned up after the storm, but somehow the apparent mess has stayed, has escaped every civic broom. There are homes worth literally a million dollars less than half a mile from here, belonging to the heirs to some of the nation's largest fortunes. There have been repeated efforts over the years by some of the homeowners to "do something" about Poseyville: to zone it out of existence, or buy it out — but the Poseys have maintained a state of such continued and puzzled refusal to every offer, that even the most persistent reformer has given up.

"What would a fellow want an old place like this for? . . . Where would we go? . . . It would be too much trouble to move that old boat. I don't know if she could take it without parting her seams. . . . I got this place all paid for. Why get into debt for a new place I might not like? . . . Been working years on that strawberry patch. Ain't going to leave it now. . . . My brother Bill lives right across the road, and Frank right behind him. If we moved, they might not be as close. . . ."

So Poseyville persists — a collection of small houses, some of them unpainted, scattered over the fifteen or twenty acres as if they'd tumbled from a tipped bushel basket. For every home there is an outbuilding cluster: one for nets, one for baiting codfish trawls, one for tools, one for general "stuff" collected off the beach, after line storms, or from the town dumps. And every yard is cleared of grass. The bare earth, often dusted with beach sand, makes it easier to repair nets; twigs and stalks of grass do not get tangled in the twine. In every yard sits a collection of trucks, cars, nets, scallop dredges, dories, power boats, skiffs, clam rakes, harpoons, lobster traps, pumps, trap stakes, fish boxes, bushel baskets, kids' tricycles, dog houses, anchors, flag buoys, oars, eel pots, buckets, rope, and the remains of the sea: flattened horseshoe crabs, clam, oyster and scallop shells, jawbones of sharks, marlin and swordfish bills, crab claws, squashed sea robins and blowfish, giant tuna tails, and a sheen of fish scales everywhere, lending their pearly luster to a landscape that looks as if it had been raised from the ocean bottom just days before to dry out in the sun.

Poseyville persists. It does so without defiance, without debate, with scarcely an acknowledgment from those who live there that their place is a kind of innocent aberration, a square of reality surrounded by the well-tended make-believe circles of the superrich. If the Poseys are conscious of their well-heeled neighbors — and they must be — they never let on. Instead, they go about their fishing as they always have. They never talk about the architectural palaces that rise from the dunes, except as ranges which help them mark the best fishing places. "Just to the east of the windmill on the Ford place, there's a good set when the wind's easterly. . . . Watch out when you're setting in front of the Simon place. Get too close to that big window and you're likely to get hung up on the wreckage of that coal schooner."

Nonplussed by being so unnoticed, would-be reformers realized they didn't have a chance. And now that the Poseys are totally surrounded, the high rollers and big timers take a certain pride and reassurance from the settlement in their midst. There may be Rembrandts on East Hampton walls and Meissen porcelain on

Amagansett dinner tables, but the Poseys, launching their dories in the sea, driving by with a truckful of fish, walking past Main Street boutiques in their oilskins and waders, now that's real. "I tell you, Henry, it's great to see them doing things the old way, isn't it. Reminds you of what it took to get this country started."

Ever since I have joined Ted's crew, I have been treated with the same detachment. I get kidded, but it is meaningless joshing, as repetitive as the lines about beefsteak putting color in my cheeks. "Why are you fishing, Johnny, a millionaire like you?"

"Aw, he's just down here for a hobby, ain't you, Jawn. If he wanted, he could buy your rig, Ted, couldn't you Johnny. You must have a bundle put away somewhere...." Lines like that, every day, one after the other, automatic, without intent or envy — meaningless, innocent, an acknowledgment of the difference of my background, nothing more. It is a statement from the Poseys that they know about the gray house on the dunes, the white chimneys and the rest. They know, but they don't care; they really don't. They watch me row, watch me pull on the oars, haul seine, tie knots, mend nets, wash fish, shovel ice, lift boxes — that's what they watch, that's what they care about — and it is all they care about. They are purely fishermen.

After fifty years of late October mornings like this, Ted is still impatient, champing, fuming about Smiley. We stand in the road, looking west to the small house where he lives alone. We can see a light in the window; then it goes out. Ted snorts.

"About time he left. He'll be promenading in here soon, looking for some breakfast. Well, he ain't going to get any. I'm going to warm up the big truck, get started. Johnny, you and Jim take Smiley with you when he gets here. He can squeeze in. I'll take the rig to Hither Hills. The boats did good at the Point yesterday. Maybe those bass have worked around. You know how to get there, don't you, Johnny?"

"Yep. Go ahead, Cap. We'll wait for Smiley."

Sitting with Jim in the "A," close and quiet there in the dark after Ted's truck has left the yard, charging off in its own envelope of ear-shattering sound, I can see the darker shape of Smiley moving toward us along the road. With his long, black overcoat over his waders, he walks slowly, taking short steps; he looks like a dark column, teetering, but angled our way, so every teeter edges him a bit closer. There is something about Smiley I have never understood. He lives alone, unmarried, unlike any of his Posey kin. He talks about drinking as if he does it all the time, but I have learned he doesn't put away half as much as he claims. I think Ted keeps Smiley on the crew partly out of family pride; Ted must assume that if Smiley had to shift entirely for himself, he couldn't get a job.

I don't know about that. I think Smiley likes crewing for Ted. Because he is the skipper's brother, Smiley gets away with a good deal of loafing, yet he gets his full share when the checks arrive from Fulton Market. So Smiley overdoes his own incompetence, babbling more than he has to, voicing more inexplicable sentences than he otherwise might. It's a game with him — a promotion of his own weaknesses, exaggerated for effect. Smiley knows Jim and

I have him figured; the recognition is there in Smiley's twinkling eyes whenever he's playacting with us. He is well named; every time I see him in that getup, I can't help smiling. He must be the only fisherman on the entire East Coast who wears a long, black chesterfield coat to work every day. This morning, I laugh aloud as he approaches the car, his cursing and rumbling as staccato as the roll of a snare drum.

"Jesus Christ, that goddammed Ted. You'd think, by Jesus, he'd learn something, wouldn't you, after forty christly years in this business. What's he in such a hurry for, tear-assing out of the yard an hour before sunup, leaving me standing there in the middle of the road. Think he's going to catch every fish in the ocean, don't he. Well, he ain't. Now I suppose I got to go haulseine without so much as a cup of coffee for my belly. Ain't that a kick in the head."

Jim picks up a thermos. "You can have some of this on the way down, Smiley. Come on, squeeze in here with me and John."

"Yes, yes. I'm riding in style this morning. We'll get there, we'll get there. Don't hurry none. We got another half-hour before we can haul, another half-hour easy, ain't that right, Johnny?" Smiley gets in, sitting there, stiffly upright between me and Jim. It's a change for him; he usually rides in the back of Ted's truck where he often stands, just behind the cab, like the leader of the expedition surveying the route ahead. I don't know how old the man is, but looking at his face as we drive along under the street lights on the Montauk Highway I can see that he is older than I had thought. The lines are deep; the multiple folds of his eyelids blink over blue eyes bleached and battered by the years. He is an old man who has risen early on a cold, autumn morning. He is a plucky old man, denied the respect his age entitles him to, and riding along with a couple of young men who have been fishing one year to his sixty. But he doesn't complain about us, or the car, not for a moment. I ask him if he thinks we'll get any fish so far to the east.

"Can't tell, Johnny, can't never tell. Them bass don't tell us where they're going. They could be anywhere, sliding over the rocks down at the point, easing around along the beach. Ted always likes to fish to the east in October. Fish gather up at the Point, don't you know. Ted wants to be first when they come around. Ted always wants to be first."

Smiley is right. Ted is waiting for us when we pull onto the beach at Hither Hills, just to the east of the state park's public campgrounds. The silver truck is backed down; the hulking dory is poised at the sea's edge, bow pointed toward the horizon where there is just the faintest shard of light showing in the southeast. Smiley nudges me.

"Told you didn't I? Didn't I? Still too dark to set, and there's that Ted, backed right down. Jesus, that man never knows when to rest."

"Johnny, you get along over here," Ted calls. "Let's get the dory off the trailer. It's slick calm here, no sea at all. We won't need much light to set."

We get the dory off, and Peter and I stand there, ready to row, waiting for Ted to give the word. I can see the morning star shining when Ted says, "Get in, John." We make the set and are ashore before the dawn grows bright enough to hide the star. There is maybe a box of fish in the bunt.

Smiley is still talking as we reload the seine into the trailered dory. He's coiling the cork line, I load the leads as Ted eases the truck along the beach where the seine is being hanked and cleared of crabs and seaweed by Jim and Peter.

"See, Johnny, I told you there wasn't no call for that christly rush. Shit, there ain't enough fish there to pay for gas. Been anybody else but Ted, I could have had my breakfast, ain't that right Johnny? Ain't that right?"

I tell him he's right, and Smiley keeps on talking. "Now we're done here, he's going to get out of the truck and say, 'Where do we go next, boys?' cause we are as far east now as we can get. You wait, that's what he's going to say."

When the net is loaded and Jim has pulled the "A" up behind the truck, Ted climbs out of the cab.

"Well boys," he says, taking off his long-billed cap and scratching his silver hair, "Where do you want to try next?" I look at Smiley, and he's got that big grin going, the one that's full of broken and missing teeth, and he's rolling his eyes so the whites show. He is funny; that's all there is to it.

"Let's go anywhere, Cap, as long as the fish are there," Peter answers, laughing. "Let's go east."

"No sets left to the east, too many rocks," Ted says.

I had thought Smiley was just talking. I can't believe there are those miles of shoreline and no place to make one set. "You mean there is all this beach and not a single place where we can haul?"

Ted points toward the cliffs of Montauk. "Even if there was a spot, we couldn't get to it. Can't get a rig down those banks. There's just one beach. That's at Ditch Plain. There's rocks there, but sometimes they get sanded under. I have hauled Ditch Plain and had no trouble. Go back the next day, you get hung up."

The sun is up now; the breeze from the nor'west is picking up. The excitement of autumn is in the air. I look at the flat ocean and feel my heart pound at the prospect of fishing in a place untouched by any other crews. "Ted, come on, let's give it a try."

Ted is surprised at the urgency in my voice. "I don't know, Johnny. The charter boats fish off Ditch Plain, and them surf-casters are always on the beach. They don't like to see us haul seiners down there. Gives them fits if we catch fish and they don't."

"Let's try it, Ted. Just once." It is a mark of my total involvement with fishing that I am trying to persuade a man who has fished most of his life to try a haul in a place I have never seen. Peter and Jim are watching the exchange with big eyes. They are wondering how Ted is going to take the pressure from a green hand on his crew.

"OK. Let's go, then," says Ted. "Let's go find out if Johnny can smell them fish."

Smiley is restored to his spot in the big silver truck, and he waves to me and Jim as we follow behind in the "A," on our way east. As I sit there, warming in the climbing sun that is now shining full through the windshield, I decide Ted is playing a hunch as much as anything. Like all fishermen, he has superstitions, believes in omens. He is trying me on this one to see if I'm lucky.

When we pull onto the beach at Ditch Plain, I can see why few haul seiners would want to set here. The place is unlike what I know as "beach." This is no long, straight stretch of sand running as far as I can see, like the beach in front of the house with the white chimneys. This is a small crescent of sand, bracketed at both ends by rocky points. Offshore of the points, boulders rise like the backs of whales, appearing and reappearing as the swells glide past. In front of us, the beach does not drop off steeply as it does to the west; here the ground is shoal far offshore. If seas of more than three feet were running, they would break a half mile out. This morning, there are scarcely any seas. The water is clear, and I can see shadows of seaweed and rocks: dark, wavering shapes that threaten us with their mystery.

Ted is looking steadily out to sea, checking the wave patterns, trying to see through the clear water to learn if the rocks are sanded or not. We wait for his decision.

"What the hell. Let's give it a try. No weather here today. Even if we do get hung up, it'll be easy enough to pick her up and ease her over the rocks."

Two surfcasters, holding their long, whippy rods like two soldiers with spears, stand on the rocks to the east and watch us as we make the set. The arc of the seine takes in the entire stretch of sand; we leave just inside the western rocks and land next to the bouldered point to the east. Ted guides us every stroke of the way. We row ashore fast when the jack goes over. Peter jumps out, grabbing the gunwale of the dory, pulling her up on the beach with exaggerated vigor. Like me, he is brimming over with the day's energy.

As I walk to the west to begin my hauling with Jim and Smiley, I marvel at the water's clarity. The gentle, small waves are translucent, catching the sun as they rise on the horizon. I look through them, into the sea's liquid green center. A bit of silver flashes in the curve of a breaking swell, then another. I wonder if I am dazzled by the refracted sun, or if it is life I see. There, there is another, then another. This last is not merely a bit of silver; it is a striped bass. I can see the white belly, the golden shoulders, even the stripes along the bronze sides — the sun is so bright, the water so clear.

I have never seen fish in a net like this before. I begin to understand that the fish rocketing along the walls of the waves are dashing from one seine wing to the other, looking for an escape. If there are so many fish in the net that they have begun to feel crowded before we start hauling, then there must be more fish here than I have ever thought possible.

"Hey! Hey! Hey! Jim.... We got fish in here." The yelling bursts from me, like shots from a cannon. For a moment, the tumult in me is uncontrollable. I turn back to yell toward Ted and Peter. I turn to the sea, transfixed again as yet another bass cruises high in the curve of a wave. This one lunges to the very top of the crest; its tail breaks the surface, leaving a gout of white water.

"There. There. Look, did you see that!" I run toward Jim and Smiley. Jim, standing in front of the "A," is handling the rope off the winch, beginning to pull steadily on it, hauling the first of the net from the waves, watching Ted's end so both wings will come ashore evenly. Jim has his lips set in the particular way he holds them when he tries not to smile — a set I see often. He nods his head toward the jack, just now pulling through the waves, vibrant with the tension the winches have begun to exert on the seine. There, in the first two feet of the net, a bass is gilled.

"You better get down there, Cap, and give Smiley a hand," Jim says quietly. "We may have a few fish here."

I hear Peter yell from the other end. A whoop, a trumpeting. I look and see him jump, like a huge dancer in waders. He is pointing to a bass gilled, like ours, just beyond the east-end jack.

Oh Christ, I say to myself. This could be it. Don't let the net get hung. Don't let anything go wrong. I stand there, useless for minutes, rooted to the beach as I immerse myself in the moment's frantic beauty. The bass have communicated their general panic. There are no longer mere flashes of silver, watery hints of fish. Now there are constant surgings as the bass search for escape in the white water of the wash.

A wave breaks, shapes glide through its arc. The wash rolls and tumbles to the beach, and from its white, foaming canopy rise the sleek shoulders of stripers. Dorsals cut the foam like knives, spilling a wake that rises inches over the surface and sustains a vertical fragility that catches the sun, so there are bright lines of light, darting here, there, and there. Each one, I know, is a fish, each one a creature of infinite vitality. I am overwhelmed at the glory of the drama. I can not move, but merely stand and watch, afraid that the thumping of my heart will force me to my knees.

"Hey, Cap. Let's go." There is an edge to Jim's voice. I run toward Smiley, who has not yet tied the next winching knot around the seine. He is, instead, trying to tug one of several gilled bass from the meshes.

"Got a bunch. We got a bunch, Johnny. Must be mostly small fish. Wouldn't have so many gilled, otherwise. Small fish get us the best price, ain't that right, Johnny?"

I don't know what to say to Smiley. He is working as he always does, with no special effort. Is it possible that he can remain apart from this realization, this actualization of an event so many fishermen talk of, but so few ever witness? Or has this happened for Smiley so often that he is unmoved? I look through the waves once again. Those shapes in their curvings draw me like a magnet.

I could look at swimming fish forever. But now the clarity is gone. The arc of the net is inscribed there in the sea's transparent aquamarine — a dingy half-circle, slurred and soiled, muddied. I do not understand.

"What the hell? Are we mudded? Is the net hung up?" I yell at Smiley, even though I stand next to him.

"Sand rile. That's a sand rile. Must be some fish in there to make a rile like that." Smiley pulls yet another gilled bass from the twine.

A sand rile — I don't know the term, but I understand it. Incredible. The fins, the tails, the turnings, the twistings, the massed surgings of thousands of striped bass have set the very sea bottom in motion. As they do in the tumult of a violent storm, the sea sand and the water mix, kept in murky suspension by the constant, gathered force of the creatures imprisoned in the shrinking curtain of twine, pulled, inch by inch as the winches turn, toward the waterless beach.

Peter whoops again, louder now because, as the net arc tightens, the two wings come closer together.

"By hand, by hand," he yells. "Ted says by hand!"

I can't believe the instruction. "Jesus, Smiley, haul by hand? We can't move all those fish."

"Ted doesn't want to lose the set. Them damn winches. Get a bunch of fish like this, get hung up before you know it. Them winches pull the twine right apart." Smiley begins tugging on the cork line. "Come on, Johnny, we can do it. Never used to do it any other way. We ain't always had them winches, you know. Sit down there on that beach and pull on that lead line.

"Oh, feel them fish, boy. Feel them fish."

I sit on the hard, damp sand, my feet toward the sea, my shoulders bent forward over my knees and my gloved hands clasped around the lead line. I pull, my back is in it. The line strums, vibrates like a steel rail a mile away from a thundering locomotive. The compressed fish are trembling against the twine;

the message of their growing terror is here, strumming the line in my hands.

"Keep it down, Cap, keep it down." Jim is behind me, helping. Peter is on the other lead line, across from us, grunting, whooping, heaving, roaring. The fish are everywhere in the wash now. It is impossible to tell sea from creature. The two are blended in the turbulence of breaking waves and running bass. The frothing is endless, perpetual. The wash hisses like water boiling on a stove. Spray flies as if the wind were blowing a gale.

Ted's cry rasps dry over the wet sounds. "Pull, boys, pull. We got a bunch here, we got a bunch. Don't let's lose them now."

He is holding the cork line higher and higher on his side, moving further and further out into the waves, trying to keep the bass from weighing down the twine, spilling over the top like living grain from the side of a sack.

"Get down there, Smiley," Ted yells. "Get down like me. God dammit, Smiley, they're going to go over your corks. Get over there, Jim, give him a hand.

"Jesus Christ, there they go." Ted is screaming now. He is up to his chest in the waves, fish all around him. He is trying to keep the corks up, by himself, deep in the surf, almost lost in the confusion of the thumping fish, the surging swells and the now tortured twine, stretched beyond its limits by the sheer numbers of the stripers.

The bunt rolls in the wash, swelled grossly by tons of twitching bass. It is full. There is no place for the fish in the quarters to go. Ted sounds to me as if he is crying.

"They're getting out. Shit, they're going over the corks. Come on Jim, for Christ's sake, keep the corks up, keep the corks up." Ted's voice is now a hoarse scream, shrill, strange, desperate, almost unintelligible. His face is crimson under the long-billed cap. He is at the brink of dementia, so far out in the surf that the waves wet his shoulders as they rise, rippling the sodden, bulging bunt.

Smiley shakes his head, in a kind of regret as he watches his brother. Peter whoops and pulls. I keep my hands locked tight on the lead line, strumming still. Jim is in the ocean with Ted, trying to hold up the corks. The net will not move.

We can do nothing. We are at a stalemate with the fish and the sea. Small rivulets of bass escape here and there, over the corks, under the leads. Ted weeps and screams. I fear he'll have a stroke, but we are all paralyzed with the functions of our duties. None of us can let go of what he holds, otherwise all may be lost.

We hold what we have, there in the high sun of the bright October forenoon. The sea swells and surges, hisses and swirls. The bass in the quarters struggle and run; they leave, like dew from the morning grass. Now it is there, then it is gone, with no moment of departure.

As we scream, yell, whoop and curse on the Ditch Plain beach, we realize, after a while, that the bass are gone from the quarters. We have the bunt to contend with now. It is, at last, a dimension we can comprehend.

Ted comes out of the sea. He is soaked. To me it appears that he is in pain. He walks to the silver truck, starts it, turns its front end to face the sea, and, roaring in low gear, edges the front bumper directly toward the bunt.

Jim and Peter unwrap the heavy line around the truck's bumper, make it fast to the net as close as they can to the swollen bag. Ted puts the truck in reverse, the monster machine roars, jerks, bounces, and edges back slowly, slowly. The bunt, packed too tightly for the fish to wriggle or twitch, eases from the wash, moving inch by inch to harder, drier sand. Ted hauls it about twelve feet this way, then the truck begins to dig its own stopping place as the huge tires spin. Ted shuts down the engine, gets out of the cab. He does not let go of the truck, though. He hangs to the door opening on the driver's side, exhausted. I trot to him.

"Johnny, tell Jim to take the 'A' back home. See if Ding is off the beach. If he is, tell him to bring his truck and crew here to help us. We'll never get these fish off before dark by ourselves."

"All right, Ted. Are you OK?"

"It's one of my spells. It will go away, or kill me. One or t'other."

I go to tell Jim. "OK," he says, "but you better watch Ted. My father died of a heart attack one hot day, conducting on the train. Fine one minute. Boom, gone the next."

The notion that Ted has been weakened, could be hurt, is a jolt to me. I am worried as I watch Jim pull off the beach to go get Ding's crew. I tell Ted to stay in the truck while Peter and Smiley and I open the cod end and start carrying the bass, one by one, to higher ground.

There seem to be hundreds, thousands, of fish. We keep carrying them, tossing them into a growing pile in the back of Ted's truck, but the bunt seems to get no smaller. Peter sings, yells, talks to the fish as he trots back and forth in his waders, sweat running down his tanned neck. A knot of surfcasters has gathered at the point. They watch, not moving, for a spell, then two of them walk to the bunt's open end while Peter and I are at the truck. As Smiley stands there, unbelieving, the casters reach in and each takes a fish. Ted waves his hand.

"Hey," he calls. "Hey, those fish are worth something, you know." If the casters can hear, they act as if they don't. They keep walking. "What the hell, Johnny, I'm too pooped to chase them. Ain't it something what some people will do." He slumps back, leaning against the cab.

We have the truck loaded by the time Ding arrives. The bass, stiff now, dry and sand covered, are piled like stovewood. There is no more space, and Ding looks at the mound in the truck and at the bunt, still impressively full, on the beach.

"Jesus, I guess you did get a bunch. Whoever had the notion to set Ditch Plain, anyway? What are you doing this far east, Ted?"

Ted waves his hand toward me. "Johnny was the one. He wouldn't rest till we come down here."

Ding looks at me and laughs. "Shit, we'll never hear the end of that, now will we."

It is three o'clock before we get off the Ditch Plain beach. We have been up, working, for almost twelve hours with no food, and we still have the fish to wash, weigh, box and tag. We have fish in the dory along with the net and Ding's trucks are full. Ted gives us half an hour for food, and Jim and I stop at a restaurant for cheeseburgers and milk.

At 10:30, we are done. The floor of Ted's fish house is an inch deep in sand and scales. In the cool room, where shaved ice is piled in drifts on the floor, there are ninety-two boxes of striped bass, tagged for shipment to brokers at Fulton Fish Market. That's more than nine thousand pounds, almost five tons of fish. They are money fish: five to ten-pounders that bring the highest market price. We have handled more than a thousand fish, three and four times over. I figure twice that many escaped the twine. We must have had the net around more than three thousand fish — close to fifteen tons. We never could have handled them, even if we had landed them all. At thirty-five cents a pound for what we did catch, I figure each share could be as high as $500.

Five hundred dollars for one day. I can not believe it, but, borne on some manic frenzy for more, I wonder as I leave if I'll be able to stir at four the next morning. I ask Ted what time he wants us.

He is sitting on the concrete steps, under the light, his gray head down on his arms. When he looks up at me, I can see the same sort of oldness in his eyes that I had seen in Smiley's.

"I, I may not be going, boys," he says to me and Jim and Peter. "I don't want another of them spells. One more, and I might have to stay off the beach for too long.

"If it's weather, you can take the rig. Jim can drive the truck. Take Smiley. The four of you can handle it. You ain't going to get another bunch like today. Ain't likely.

"Supposed to breeze up tomorrow, anyway. You might get one set in the morning. If you want, take the rig. You won't have to go far. Right down here to the radio towers will be as good as any. You'll never get Ditch Plain. Ding has already got his crew down there. He didn't get nothing to the west today. They'll spend the night on the beach to keep that Ditch Plain set."

"OK, Cap," says Jim. "We'll be by. We'll see what the weather is like."

I can see no stars the next morning; the breeze is not from the northwest, it is from the east, bringing with it the wetness and sounds of the sea. Ted's light is not on. Peter arrives as Jim and I sit there in the "A," then Smiley shows up. I marvel to myself at the way this man in his seventies can endure. Jim climbs into the big silver truck, starts it, and I follow in the "A."

The southeast chop has not had time to build, we discover

when we reach the beach at Napeague, opposite the radio towers. Working on an ocean flattened by days of wind off the land, the stiffening breeze generates short seas that topple almost as soon as they are formed. In the gloomy dawn, the ocean is dotted with gobs of white, but there are no swells rolling ashore. It will be hard rowing, but we can set with no trouble.

None of us wants to. I have that feeling standing by the dory with Peter, waiting for Jim to leave the truck. We are exhausted from the day before, numb. But none of us will admit it; each of us dreads learning from the other crews that we missed a good fishing morning by not making a set. Besides, if the wind stays in the east, there's a chance there won't be fishing weather for several days. That's when we will get our rest; at least that's what we say to ourselves, there by the ocean on this lowering morning.

Jim and Smiley come down to the boat.

"Smiley can make the set," Jim says.

I am surprised. "Why not you, Cap?"

"Smiley doesn't know how to drive. We need someone in the truck."

"Don't worry, Johnny, don't worry. I know what I'm doing. I know. You think I been on this beach as long as I have and I can't set a net." Smiley hunches up his coat and gets ready to clamber over the gunwales as Peter and I get in and Jim pushes off. It's lucky no seas are running. We bend the oars trying to pull against the chop; the dory founders as if she has a sea anchor dragging. Peter grunts, strains, but finds enough cheer somewhere in him to yell, "It looks fishy to me, Cap, it looks fishy to me. We'll get around another ninety boxes."

Smiley is slow setting. He takes small handfuls of the lead line; doesn't, or can't, throw them far enough. Peter and I are rowing the net overboard — pulling hard enough so the forward motion of the dory pulls the net into the water. With the net still wet and sandy from the day before, the rowing is slow, hard, labored. I can feel myself tiring fast, and I wish, more than anything, for the set to end.

We reach the bunt. We are halfway there. Peter and I stop rowing, leaning on our oars, waiting for Smiley to heave the bag and the buoy. It is his only function, really. Neither Peter nor I is fully certain of the way the bunt and the buoy must be arranged to fish properly.

Neither, it turns out, is Smiley. We are losing ground on the set as the onshore wind pushes at the dory and the chop slaps on her beam, jostling her back toward the beach. The seine arc is flattening.

"Smiley, come on," says Peter, leaning toward the stern from his oars amidships, but not wanting to stand in the boat that is pitching and rolling now that we have no headway.

Smiley stands there, studying the twine, his gloved fingers fluttering over the bunt as if he could read a braille code there that would instruct him. He picks up the buoy, starts to flip the rope one way, then another. I know now that he has forgotten, or never knew, the proper way.

He can not fool himself or us any longer.

He picks up the bunt. The heavy twine drapes down the front of his black overcoat. He grunts with effort.

"Shit. I'll throw the goddamn thing. It's gotta be OK. Ain't that right, Johnny?"

Smiley swings his armful of twine back, then heaves the heavy netting toward the horizon. As he does, the dory pitches, wallows, then rolls.

Smiley and the bunt go over the gunwale together. For a second or so, the air under his overcoat keeps him up. I am looking into his pale face, white there in the dark sea. His thin hair is spread in the water, the way it was the first day I saw him in the back of Ted's truck.

He doesn't cry out. There is no time. The bunt, with its extra lead weights and rings in the cod end, sinks fast. Smiley goes under with it. Nothing marks his going. The chop beats at the side of the boat as Peter and I sit there, paralyzed with our comprehension of what is happening.

Peter moves first. He stands, lunges for the net, starts hauling the bunt back in the dory. He heaps it, dripping, in the bottom, hauls further back, first to the quarters, then to the wing. Smiley does not surface with the netting. The dory is sloppy now with the sea water the net has shed. We roll in the chop. I can see Jim standing, still, on the beach.

"Should we go over?" I ask Peter. "I can strip and swim."

"No, too deep here. Besides, the net is down there. You can get tangled in that."

"Peter, Peter, what can we do?" I am trembling, shaking, shivering. I want to vomit.

We sit there, stupidly, in the rolling dory. It's as if we are waiting for the miracle, for Smiley to surface, shed of his coat and waders, to swim toward us like a summer swimmer, and clamber over the side of the boat, the way I used to climb over the sides of the *Emma,* playing with my brother Chick.

The gray sea hisses in the wind.

"We can't do a thing," Peter says, thumping down in his seat. "We can't haul the net back. We'll sink the dory. We've got to go ahead, finish the set, get this twine out of the boat. How else are we going to get ashore? We may not make it now, with the wind breezing up all the time.

"Come on, John. We better row."

We bend to the oars. The seine slides over the gunwale, cork by cork, lead by lead. When we turn the corner and the wind is on our stern, Peter stands and heaves great handfuls of lead line overboard. With the chop pushing the boat toward shore, I can row alone now.

We don't stop when we approach the beach. I row, Peter hangs on to the line and we surf ashore sloppily on the shoulders of one of the small seas. Jim is there waiting. He grabs the dory bow, runs a line through the bow ring. He runs to the truck, backs it, and jerks the dory to high ground. He has said nothing since we came ashore.

Peter walks with me to the far wing. We are helped by the southeast wind and, somehow, we get the seine ashore; Jim works his end single-handed, running from the winch to tie on his own hauling line. There are maybe three boxes of bass in the bunt. Smiley did have it set up right.

We haul the bunt up on the beach and stand around it, looking at the fish. Jim breaks his silence. He looks at me and Peter with his hard, blue eyes and asks, "Who will tell Ted?"

What the hell happened to yesterday? That's what I want to know as I look up and down the long, empty, windy beach. What the hell happened to the excitement, the good times? How did it get like this — the three of us, here with this wet, sand-heavy seine to pick up, with this lumbering dory to load, alone here on this raw morning without any sun? How could we have worked so hard, come all this way to be in the boat when Smiley goes overboard, when Ted's brother drowns, with us in the boat? What in the christly hell are we doing here? We don't belong here. And Smiley is gone — the old guy that I liked so, the fool who was never a fool. And now we have to decide who will tell Ted. God.

The wind picks up as we load the net. There will be no fishing this afternoon, nor tomorrow. That thought eases our depression a bit as we finish our work on the beach and begin the mournful procession back to Ted's — Jim driving the truck with Peter beside him; me alone in the "A," still seeing Smiley's presence in the empty seat next to me, still in a kind of shock as the realization of the loss works deeper into me.

Ted is sitting on the steps, waiting as we roll into the yard, the clamshells and scallop shells crunching under the tires. He walks over and peers into the back of the truck when Jim stops and shuts off the roaring engine. Ted glances at the sand-covered pile of bass, makes his eyeball appraisal.

"About three boxes. Well, could have been worse. Breeze up too much for another set, did it?"

Jim is the one who answers. He waits a long moment before he does. "Yes, Cap. Blowing hard now, from the southeast. That's the end of fishing today, tomorrow too, the way it looks.

"But we would have come back anyway, Ted." Jim walks closer; his face is inches from Ted's. "We had an accident, Ted. Smiley, well, Smiley went overboard, trying to heave the bunt. He stumbled. A sea hit the boat. He just went, Ted. We couldn't do a thing."

Ted stands there, nodding. "It happens, boys. It happens. My nephew, Arthur, drowned last spring putting in trap stakes. Fell from his sharpie. Drowned in a few feet of water. Couldn't swim a stroke. Neither could Smiley, neither can I."

He turns to walk to the house, then stops, turns back. "You didn't find him, did you?"

Jim shakes his head.

Ted climbs the steps, turns back to us again. "Wash and pack them fish. I got to call my brothers. We'll have to have a service of some sort." He steps inside, shuts the door, leaving us standing there in the yard, listening as the southeast wind rumbles with the sound of the surf, breaking harder now against the beach a mile from where we are. In the sound, I see Smiley going over the gunwale. He's out there now, somewhere, I tell myself as we walk toward the fish house to finish the day's work.

There is no fishing the next day, or the next. The wind backs into the northeast and stays there — mean, cold, and wet — too rough even for the scallopers.

Because of the weather, nearly every Posey in town is at Smiley's service. They crowd in the pews at the church, dressed mostly in dark suits that I have never seen before, and wearing heavy, black shoes. The ruddy faces look even ruddier indoors, and the hands holding the prayer books seem huge, swollen so by the sea that the stiff, broad fingers have a difficult time turning the thin pages. The service is short, somber. The men file out, not talking. Ted comes over to me.

"I'll call you when it's weather," he says. That's all.

It is November before we can fish again. The northeast wind held for two more days after Smiley's service, then blew southeast for a day before finally turning northwest once again, bringing back clear skies and knocking down the heavy surf that had built steadily during the storm.

It takes a while after a blow for the ocean to settle down. The four of us — me, Jim, Peter and Ted — can set on the first afternoon of the first clear day, but the seas are still significant, coming in hard, sharp and murky. When we haul the net, it comes ashore dirty. Bits of debris are caught in almost every foot of twine; it takes us an extra hour to pick the meshes clean. If I were the skipper, I wouldn't bother setting so soon after a storm, but the Poseys don't make choices about when to fish and when not to. They go whenever they can launch their dories through the surf; sometimes they try even when they should not. There are many stories about dories being flipped and pitchpoled in the surf — just as many tales of disaster as there are about success at unlikely times, such as this breezy afternoon in early November with the sea the color of coffee.

But we score no success. Our two sets are dry hauls; there is nothing in the bunt. It comes ashore like a long, empty sleeve, and I am glad when the sun sets and we head off the beach. The western sky is tinged with green at dusk — a signal that Jim and I both recognize from our previous winter of wood cutting. Riding home in the "A" I remind him.

"See that, Cap? See that green sky? We'd better wear our longjohns tomorrow, or we'll freeze our ass for sure."

"Yes, yes," says Jim, but he goes no further with the banter. There hasn't been much talk since Smiley's drowning. We are a working crew now, not a laughing crew, not a crew of friends. We are merely four fishermen, going through the motions, waiting together for the memories to ease.

The first revival of Jim's spirit, and Peter's for that matter, comes the next morning after Ted backs down and we drop the dory off the trailer at the edge of the ocean, ready for the dawn set. Jim leans over the gunwale, picks up the bailer and starts cracking the ice in the boat's bilges. He nudges Peter.

"Look at that, Cap. You want to watch that ice. When Ted tells you, 'Get in, Peter,' you're liable to go flying." He thumps the bailer down again, grunting. "Must have been some cold to freeze that salt water. Well, maybe it's cold enough to move a pod of them bass along this way. We could use a haul one of these days. December will be here before we know it."

"Don't talk about it, Jim, don't talk about it," Peter says. "I don't want to even think about December yet. All I want to think about is fish."

We make the set on a cold, calm sea that reminds me of the first days Jim and I fished together, with Swede, in his dory at the Main Beach. It was still and cold on those mornings.

I can see every cork on the seine as I walk west to help Jim. My imagination is working: I persuade myself that there are at least fifteen boxes of bass inside the half-circle. But I don't say anything to Jim. There is no sign that we have fish. No stripers are gilled, there are no swirlings in the surf, no breaks flashing on the flat sea. But my anticipation persists. I am glad, in a way, to feel my heart thumping again.

By the time the extra corks on the bunt buoy are just in back of the surf and the quarters are coming through the wash, I know that my hope is wishful thinking. There just is not enough activity in the water to indicate that we have any fish, much less fifteen boxes.

But as the winching stops and we go to hand-haul the bunt ashore, I feel a kind of weight on the line. Perhaps we haven't made a dry haul after all. Then I see a shadow in the surf, a darkness in the net's cod end. I yell.

"There's one. We got something."

The next sea breaks, moves the bunt further ashore, then recedes, leaving the bag almost dry — dry enough for me to see what we have caught. I recognize Smiley's long, black overcoat, there in our net. I want to be someplace else, anyplace.

We keep hauling. There is nothing else we can do. After six days, the sea has given us back Smiley. I don't want to look. I want to run, I want to stop trembling, I want Ted and Peter and Jim to disappear. I want the sea to take back what it has brought us. I want this entire, wretched, sickening time to be wiped from my memory, from my mind, from my life.

"Jesus, oh Jesus." Ted says it softly, on his sighing breath. I hear it, and then I hear the rumble of trucks. Ding and his crew are coming from the east, toward us. I am relieved by that. Ding will know what to do.

Ted calls, "Johnny. Come on, Johnny. Help me carry him to the truck. Come on. Help me."

Ted opens the cod end, loosens the rope that runs through the rings. He and I hold the feet of Smiley's waders while Peter and Jim pull the bunt away from him. Jim comes down and takes one rubber-covered ankle, I take the other. Ted goes to the other end, wraps his arms around the black overcoat just below the armpits and lifts. I keep my eyes on the black rubber foot in my hands as we walk to the big silver truck and slide Smiley in the back. I am surprised at how heavy he is. I would have thought not much would be left after six days in the water.

Ding's truck pulls up alongside and Ding looks down from the cab into Ted's truck, but he says nothing. Ted climbs into the silver truck, starts the engine and lumbers off the beach. Ding turns his truck off and climbs down. He yells back at his crewman Lindy. "Come on, let's give these fellows a hand loading."

We get the dory on the trailer, and all of us pull the net toward it, ready for loading. Ding and I are across from each other, he pulling on the cork line, me on the leads. The sun is high now, bright, spilling some warmth onto the beach. I don't know what to say. I don't want to talk about Smiley, about anything to do with this day.

"Ding," I say, "tell me, what did you get that morning after you waited all night to make that Ditch Plain set?"

Ding stopped pulling, surprised. "You never heard about that? We didn't set. Couldn't. The surfcasters were there, shoulder to shoulder, lined up from one end of that beach to the other. Somebody sure gave them the word. I wasn't going to take a chance in that place with those bastards on the beach. No telling what they would have done.

"We left. Went west and made the Gurney's set. Got about eight boxes, is all."

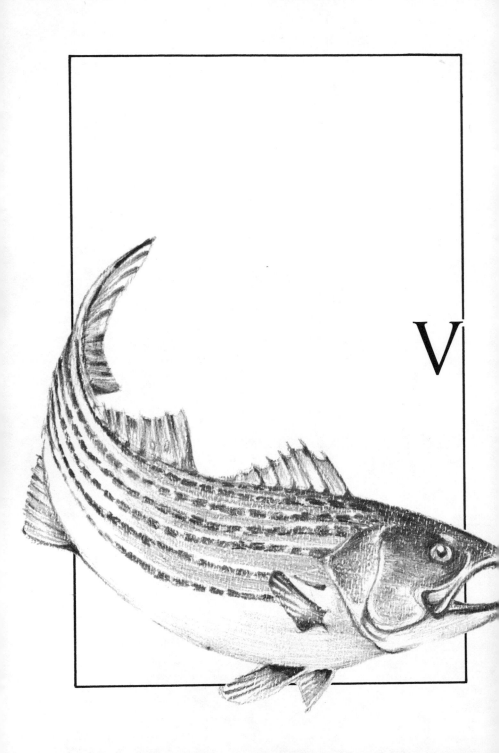

V

Shortly after the Civil War, a small but uniformly prosperous group of gentlemen organized several clubs along the nation's northeast coast. The chief purpose of the effort was to develop facilities for catching the striped bass on rod and reel. Communicating frequently with one another via a rather elaborate messenger service employing carrier pigeons, the gentleman anglers shared information on the whereabouts of their quarry. During the fishes' spring and fall migrations one can assume that the airways were clogged with pigeons racing from club to club with reports of good fishing here, or poor fishing there.

The clubs faded after the turn of the century as striper populations reached a cyclical ebb. The large, heavy, calcutta cane rods — adapted from European salmon fishing rods — and the wooden-sided reels used by the gentleman fishermen were put away, or modified for use with other, more available fish.

During the late 1920s and early 1930s, as the number of American "gentlemen" was painfully abridged by the financial chaos of the 1929 bank closings and the stock market collapse, mysterious but natural events combined to restore the East Coast striper to nineteenth century levels of abundance.

As gentlemen watched their numbers dwindle in the marble corridors of Manhattan's finance palaces, the surging waters off Long Island's Montauk Point, 120 miles to the east, were becoming populated with vast numbers of stripers, and, in spite of their money troubles, the hardier sportsmen of the city discovered a kind of respite from the stock market in the pursuit of the fish that lived in the shadow of Montauk's cliffs. At first, however, the equipment that had served well in the quieter waters and tidal estuaries where the clubs had once been, could not be modified to function in the fierce surf that surged so steadily around the Point's rocky beaches.

Two steps were taken to solve the problem. One enterprising fisherman carefully wrapped a heavy, linen line around pegs set in a box, then, standing on the beach in the waves' wash, swung a shiny bit of tin-coated lead, with a hook fitted to it, from one end of the coiled line. Twirling the "tin squid" around his head in wider and wider circles, as a hammer thrower might, the fisherman strained to generate maximum centrifugal force. When he reached his limits, he released the line, the tin squid flew out toward the open sea, pulling the coiled line with a hiss from the box on the beach. As soon as the lure hit the water, the fisherman began retrieving it, hand over hand, pulling the shiny lure through the waves where it could catch refracted sunlight and gleam as brightly as a herring or mackerel. Seen by a striper feeding in the surf, the tin squid might trigger a strike and the angler on the beach would be fast to his quarry.

Those hand-heavers were the first surfcasters. But even as they worked from North Bar, Caswell's, Cocoanuts and the other small, stony Montauk beaches that curve into the base of the cliffs like a bit of random embroidery on the land, other determined fishermen defied the Atlantic itself with constructions that had not been seen before and have not been seen since. As if the ocean swells were somehow insignificant and the seasonal storms would never occur, men for whom hand-heaving was neither sporting nor fashionable pooled what resources they had salvaged, and had local carpenters build casting piers — long, narrow, zigzag walkways of wooden planks supported by pilings that had somehow been placed within the very heart of the rocks over which waves draped their foaming veils.

Marring the Point's natural symmetry like broken toothpicks in a pear, the single-plank platforms were built wherever their planners and builders could find submerged purchase. Like the clubs which had preceded them by fifty years, the slim, crooked fingers of wood poking into the Atlantic were the property of those who had financed their construction, and their guests. The fishermen gained a great advantage from these walkways that jutted out so far into the surf that bass often rolled in the sea at the very base of the platform pilings.

During the 1930s, casting piers were a part of the Montauk seascape. Damaged and often totally destroyed by the storms of autumn, winter, and spring, the platforms were stubbornly rebuilt by those early surfcasters whose compulsion to put themselves closer to striped bass not only pushed some of them deeper into debt, but also brought on the injury and even death of several gentlemen who slipped on the slick, wet wood and fell into the breaking sea below.

Given such hazards, and the expense, the number of surfcasters at Montauk and other similar locations from Hatteras to Cape Cod was not to become significant until after another event as traumatic to the human community as the crash of '29. This time it was World War II. In addition to tanks, bombsights, and nuclear fission, the war's demands for technological innovation made what fishermen survived the holocaust the beneficiaries of such reasonably priced discoveries as steel-and-fiberglass rods, synthetic monofilament line, molded plastic lures, bakelite-sided, open-faced spinning reels, neoprene waders, insulated thermal underwear, battery packs, dehydrated food, and four-wheel-drive vehicles. The postwar economic vitality allowed many factory workers the wherewithal to purchase every new accoutrement of the well-equipped surfcaster.

After the war, any person who was spotted on North Bar

twirling a tin squid attached to a line coiled in a pegged box, would have been taken away to have his sanity calibrated. By the mid-1940s, the casting platforms that had been built so adventurously and so expensively less than two decades before had become memories only; photographs of them that appeared every now and then in the *East Hampton Star* were viewed with gentle ridicule by Grumman assembly line workers down from Bethpage on a fishing trip. Blessed with a return of the striped bass, and the equipment magic the consumer-oriented manufacturers were working on his behalf, the surfcaster of the postwar period emerged as one of the newest, most determined, and proprietary elements in the recreational fishing patterns that were evolving and would become a major socioeconomic presence along the coasts of the entire nation, but most particularly wherever the striped bass rolled and swirled in the inshore waters of the Atlantic.

From the handful of nineteenth century gentlemen who had organized the interclub carrier pigeon network of striped bass bulletins, to the intrepid and foolhardy builders of Montauk's rickety casting platforms, the process of catching a striped bass by tossing a lure into the sea from the shore had by the 1950s been stripped of most of its mystery and inaccessibility by the forces of technology, prosperity, and a flourishing democracy which brought an end to notions that rod-and-reel fishing with artificial lures was merely a gentlemen's avocation.

The turnabout was swift and aggressive. Encouraged by a number of newly arrived publications created to meet informational appetites of the growing tens of thousands of casters, surf fishermen organized rapidly. And it was only natural for them to find a kind of fraternity in their particular fishing form. In spite of the moderating effects of new kinds of rods and reels and better waterproof clothing, surfcasting remained a rugged recreation, and, as always, it was in the intensity of their shared discomforts that the surfcasters of the fifties formed the organizational bonds which changed the immediate fate of their favorite trophy — the striped bass.

There are obvious penalties to be paid by anyone who stands in the surf through the worst weather of spring, summer and fall. At Montauk, certainly, the water temperature is often cold, the rocks beneath the wash are slippery, seaweed covered, and the advancing swells, spawned by winds, earthquakes and other meteorological phenomena, can be erratic and quite unpredictable. Standing in the sea, allowing the water to ride waist high, within a few inches of his wader tops, a fisherman who must keep both hands on his twelve-foot casting rod is likely to be swept off his feet by a surprise wave, or, at the very least, to have his waders filled. Many surfcasters, in their desire to get a few feet closer to where they believe the bass to be, will stand their ground as breaking seas thrash almost at head height.

When he is driven from his casting spot by exhaustion and chill, the surfcaster often must take his rest on the beach, must learn to live with the grit of the sand and the shelterless plain that provides no hiding place from the wind. And, because the striped bass is primarily a nocturnal feeder, the surfcaster must also endure darkness as one of the standard fishing environments. Thus a Grumman worker and his friends, off to Montauk for a recreational weekend, will arrive late Friday afternoon, fish until Saturday's dawn, sleep in fitful naps on the beach during the day, and then fish again through Sunday's dawn. In the process, the surfcaster makes hundreds of casts requiring strength, coordination, surefootedness, resistance to numbing temperatures, and a patience so persistent that even though he may not catch or sight a fish, the caster will continue his lonely work through the darkest predawn hours, in spite of broken lines, malfunctioning reels, snagged lures, and fingers swollen from immersion.

In addition to being the least comfortable of any fishing form, surfcasting is also one of the least productive. Restricted to the arc of his casts, the beach fisherman has a most limited range. To be caught, the fish must first swim within the small quadrant the caster can cover, then it must decide whether to strike the lure.

The combined variables generally guarantee the surfcaster a relatively small catch. One or two striped bass to show for a night's fishing would be considered a good take by most casters. So many days and nights are spent fishing with no reward that many experienced surfcasters learn to expect nothing when they embark on their expeditions.

Hostile environments and small catches, however, have evidently not been enough to dissuade some two million casters who populated the fishery at the start of the seventies. It costs little, once outfitted, to fish as a caster: studies show that the average daily spending rate is in the neighborhood of ten dollars per fisherman. Casters need no equipment but rod, reel, line, and lure — plus waders if they want to stay reasonably dry. They can fish from any beach they can reach; they are not at the mercy of rough seas like their boating counterparts; and they are, at all times, in position at the lip of the sea, that place of eternal romance.

The shared mystery of dark nights in that place, the mutual hardships and discomforts of dawns and dusks on the beach, together with the recognized sportsmanship of their particular kind of fishing has united surfcasters as few other recreational groups are united. Their fraternities abound, and, although individual fishermen say the size of their catch is not personally significant, the primary thrust of every surfcasting club and organization has been toward improving the surfcaster's chances of bringing home more and larger fish.

These surfcasters are primarily blue-collar Americans. They understand the power of united action; they are conditioned to what they see as the short end of several sticks — the housing stick, the pay-scale stick, and the social stick. The notion that although they earn more than a bank clerk they are still regarded as a different class of citizen, bothers blue-collar workers, builds resentments and aggressions which are quick to surface. Thus, when a surfcaster who has been fishing vainly through the night watches as haul seiners pull in two tons of striped bass, his chagrin is predictable. Given the assumptions fostered by his "short-end" conditioning, the caster is also likely to assume that it is the seiners and their catches that are the reason for his denial. The facts of the matter have yet to persuade the casters otherwise. Even though recreational fishermen (about half of them surfcasters) combined to take some fifty million pounds of striped bass and bluefish in the single year of 1970, while commercial netters took ten million pounds of the same two species in the four years from 1969 through 1973, the surfcaster has been determined to end the netting of striped bass ever since the first casting clubs were organized shortly after World War II technology allowed the popularization of beach fishing.

There has not been a legislative session in Albany since the early 1950s without its delegation of striped bass fishermen arguing for new laws which would outlaw seining. The so-called "bass bills" have become perennial, and recently have lost by narrowing margins. The Long Island seiners owe their survival to Perry Duryea, one of Albany's most powerful Republican legislators, a gubernatorial candidate and an East Ender of several generations whose family earned its now considerable wherewithal in the commercial fishing business. Without Duryea's power and allegiance to his fishing heritage (as well as his common-sense analysis of catch totals), Long Island's commercial bass catch would be a memory, just as it is in Connecticut, Massachusetts, Rhode Island, New Hampshire, and Maine.

Because New York is the northernmost state without an anti-netting law, and because so many of the organized surfcasters live in and around the New York City suburban complex, the tension in that state is relentless. Each year, forgetting that they share hard lives as working people, the surfcasters and the seiners clash. Several times, nets have been cut; vandalism to gear left (as tradition would have it) on the beach, has been brutal. There have been fist fights, threats, endless cursings, and, on occasion, haul seiners have purposely set their nets "around" surfcasters on the beach, forcing them to stop casting and find other locations.

And it is not only seiners who are the targets of the surfcasters' apparently abundant wrath. When charter boats and private boats maneuver too close to Montauk's North Bar, searching inshore for the same striped bass the surfcaster strains to reach from the rocky beach, their skippers must always be on the alert for a tin squid or a treble-hooked plug cast like a projectile toward the wheelhouse, or arched across the trolled lines so when it is retrieved, the surfcaster's lure will tangle, or break, the boat's fishing lines.

Because the nation's surfcasters spend more than $2 billion annually, they are seldom without the finances for their fight. Sporting goods retailers and wholesalers; manufacturers of the "go-anywhere" vehicles that carry the casters along beaches and over dunes; the motel and hotel chains that house and feed them when they leave the beach; the breweries who make the beer that sustains them before, after, and during their fishing — these commercial entities and others are quick to bankroll their best customers, no matter what the cause.

Nurtured inwardly by the shared miseries of their chosen fishing technique, and outwardly by the business that prospers from their annual expenditure of $2 billion, surfcasters spend raw and gritty nights on the beach, dreaming of the giant striped bass that lurks in the surf and also fantasizing the day when the great fish will become exclusively their prey, which is quite likely the way the gentlemen of those nineteenth century clubs viewed the sole object of their pursuits: the striped bass.

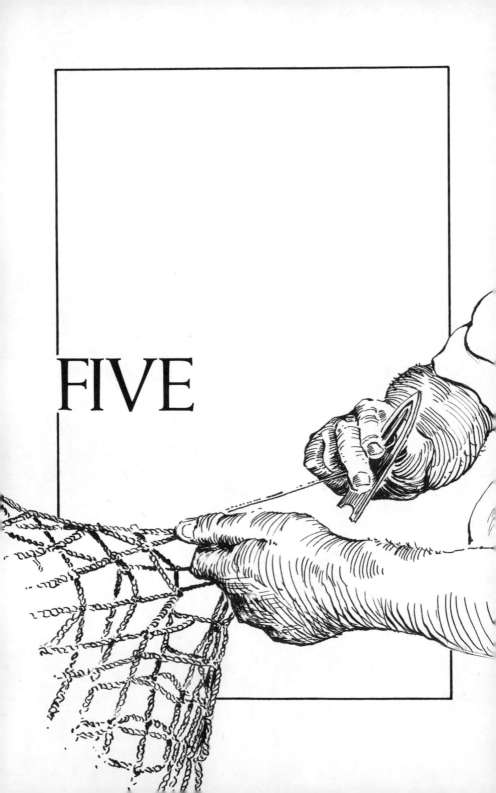

FIVE

It surprises me to hear Ding say that surfcasters stopped him from making his set. He is one of the most bullheaded, big voiced of the Poseys. There is a substratum of belligerence behind the rawboned grin, the ruddy face and the stiff blond hair. I would never tease Ding into a fight; he'd be there before I expected it, fists clenched. It must have been a strain on his self-control to abandon the Ditch Plain set after he and most of his crew had spent the raw night on the sand so they would be certain of being the first on the beach at dawn. I want more reasons.

"I can't believe that, Ding. Why would a Posey give way to a bunch of surfcasters? What could they do to you, anyway?"

The last of the net goes into the dory. We have finished the loading job. Ding taps the top of the seine, lays the jack and the coils of the inshore line on the twine mound, looks at me. "They cut Bobby's net right in two. He was hauling up to Southampton, surfcasters went out in one of those little tin boats they have, picked up the twine right near the bunt and just hacked that net in two. Then they took off, landed down the beach where some of their buddies were waiting in a jeep. Bobby lost the whole set.

Never did find out who cut the twine. Took half a day to mend it."
Climbing down from the dory Ding comes over closer, puts his face
inches from mine.

"Besides, Ted says we can't cause no aggravation. Them bastards will be up in Albany in January, looking to put us out of
business. They do it every year. Want the whole ocean to themselves. Ted says if we was to start any trouble, they might get the
politicians down on us. Way it is now, with Ted and his friends
from up the island, them casters haven't been able to get the law.

"If I'd wanted to set, I would have set. Them casters ain't
going to keep me from it. I didn't want no trouble, is all. Ted
would have been some upset, this close to January. Besides, what
with Smiley going over while we was down there, I'm glad now I
didn't try that morning. What happened to Smiley was trouble
enough. Ted might have had a real bad spell if I'd come back from
Ditch Plain on the same morning and told him we'd tangled with
the casters. That might a been all it took to put Ted down."

He opened the door on the passenger side of his truck. "Come
on," he said, "leave the rig here. It'll be OK. Somebody will come
back with Ted's truck to haul it home. You ride back with me. I
suppose now that Smiley has turned up, there won't be much fishing
till we get him proper buried.

"That was something, wasn't it, him turning up in the seine
like that. It ain't the first time, though, it ain't the first time. Bodies
a'plenty come ashore during the war, some of them tangled in gill
nets, some washed up on the beach, and one or two in a haul seine.
A while back, one of them Edwards boys went overboard off his
father's whaleboat. Turned up in the old man's haul seine two
days later. Funny how the ocean works.

"I expect Ted is better off with Smiley back. Don't seem proper
not to have a place in the Posey plot, once you're gone. Better in
the ground than alone out there in all that water." Ding waves his
arm at the horizon as we pull off the beach and start down the road
to Poseyville.

Smiley is buried the next day. The same men in the dark suits with their outdoor faces and big hands who had been at the church service a week before stand around the grave while the minister says the words and throws a handful of dirt on the wooden coffin. Ted stops me on the way back to the car, putting his hand on my arm.

"Johnny, we can still go fishing, you know." His voice is not loud, but there is a competitive edge to it. Smiley was right about Ted. He wants to catch fish more than anything, and he wants to catch more than any of his brothers. "I mean, you fellows know what you're doing now, you and Jimmy and Peter. The four of us can handle it. We'll only fish when it's weather. Used to be we never had no more than four to a crew.

"We should finish out the season, don't you think? Probably another hundred boxes out there, just waiting for us. Ain't that right, Johnny?"

"I guess so Ted, I guess so. What about Jim and Peter? What do they say?"

"You talk to them, Johnny, will you? They probably want to keep going. Too late to do much else now. If you talk to them, they'll come along."

I'm not so sure that Ted is right about me being able to persuade Jim. In spite of the big haul, I have gotten the notion during the past week or so — ever since Smiley went over — that Jim is about ready to quit fishing. For some reason I haven't figured out, he seems to find it difficult to work with Ted, or anybody, for that matter. Off and on through the fall he has talked with me about a small haul seine that could be handled by one man with a helper. "You might not get such big hauls," he would tell me, "but you could fish your own way and you wouldn't have to split the shares with so many others." I have just about decided that Jim won't be content until he tries it. He has this compulsion to go it alone, to do it his way. I tell myself it has something to do with his having been a fighter pilot, up there, alone over the Sahara during the early part of the war. A man would have to like being on his own to do that.

But Jim doesn't hesitate. When I tell him Ted wants the four of us to keep going, he says he'll be there in the morning. And Peter of course, Peter is ready to go back to work anytime. He's banging away at the side of his house when I stop by, putting up shingles, slamming the hammer down, hustling the shingles into position, humming, moving fast, with that incredible zest for work that gushes from the internal fountain that is so uniquely Peter's.

"Sure, Cap, sure. I'll be there. I'm ready for another bunch, aren't you? We'll get one too, Jawn. We'll get one. You just wait and see."

As I leave the driveway, Peter waves goodbye, holding his hammer high, yelling, "We'll get 'em, we'll get 'em!"

We try, that's for sure.

The four of us work as hard as I have ever worked during the next three weeks. With the equinoctial storms gone by, we get a spell of decent weather through the end of November that has me wishing for a stormy day or two just so I can get some rest.

But the fishing weather holds. The days are gray, cold, but still. No wind blows under the November clouds. The ocean rests, as steady as a pewter plate under the gray sky. Small waves slap at the beach; the sea water gets heavier as it get colder, the slapping seas are sharper than they would be in summer, but they are no threat to us or Ted's cumbersome dory.

I row the bow oars, Peter amidships, and Ted sets the net while Jim handles the winches and the "A," and catches our bow when we come ashore. We make four or five sets a day, always two in the morning, two in the afternoon, and, if there are any fish at all, one in the middle of the day when we otherwise might quit for lunch and a rest.

We have worked together long enough now so that our jobs have become routine. Back the truck down, roll off the dory, get in John, get in Peter, pull, row around, toss the bunt, come ashore, jerk the dory up with the truck, winch in the seine until the bunt buoy is in back of the surf, pull the bunt ashore by hand, take out the fish, reload the seine in the dory, start the process over until the day is done and we get back to Ted's at dusk when we wash, weigh, ice, box, and tag the fish, say goodnight, see you in the morning, and back the next dawn about five A.M.

For the first time since I began this fishing adventure, I find myself thinking of it as a job. It is a job I like. I am still fascinated by the sea, still aware of the ripples of anticipation I feel with each set, still able to hope for a big haul. But I am also weary. I wonder how the weather pattern can persist, and I wonder how much longer we can keep hauling for a box or two of striped bass on each set. We end the days with four or five boxes, sometimes less, sometimes a bit more. We're making about twenty-five or thirty dollars for a fourteen-hour day. It's nothing to complain about, nothing to cheer about. It's work, that's what it is, and I begin to make the time go more easily by building dreams of a good haul — thirty or forty boxes of bass, a haul the four of us can handle without extra help, but a haul large enough to set our hearts to pounding the way they did that day at Ditch Plain.

The day after Thanksgiving, the weather pattern collapses. Instead of a flat, pewter ocean, there is a great steely presence — a wild, rolling sea, pushed into heaving hills of water topped with white manes blown wild by a southeast gale that leaps at the dunes the way a lion springs at its prey.

At last, some time off. Some time to try to shed the grit of the sand, the sweetness of the smell that fish leave on my clothes. Fishing from a boat at sea has its dangers and discomforts, but they do not include sand. Haul seining from the beach is an occupation that mixes sand and salt water in equal parts, makes them constant presences in a fisherman's days and many of his nights. The sand on these East End beaches is fine, white, and compounded of hard rock formations, like granite, quartz, and various schists. It is abrasive, gritty, and yet fine enough to be blown around by a breeze.

My wadered feet sink in it, my scalp collects it; sand gets in my crotch, under my nails, in the pockets of all my clothes, and in the very food I eat. After a run of good weather like this November when fishing fills days on end, sand collects in my bed so that when I fall into it at night there is no respite from the beach; it is there to surround my dreams. No amount of washing, shaking, brushing, or blowing seems to be able to get rid of the last of the sand. It becomes a part of my life, a mark of my work as common as the calluses on my palms from hauling in the net, the hands swollen from salt water, and the strangely sweet smell of the fish that clings so to my clothes and my skin.

I don't understand how the odor of fish can be so deeply absorbed. We wear waders most of the working day. We must consume this essence of fish (Jim calls it "eau de fish") by a kind of osmosis that transmutes the oils in the fish slime into a part of our own skins. It is not, for me, a disagreeable smell. Fresh fish have a kind of fruity scent, like ripe melon. It is a unique odor, one I have never smelled before, and one which I was once proud to acknowledge. When I first began fishing, the smell of my trade was witness to my participation. But now, when a southeaster keeps us from the beach, when I get the time, at least, to scour most of the sand from my bed, to shake out my waders, to repair the broken buttons on my oilcoat, to patch my boots, to put on clean clothes — I would like the transformation to include an escape from the smell. It does not. No amount of bathing, no splash of aftershave, no spray of cologne can subvert the smell of fish. The striped bass go with me to the movies.

Their redolent reminder is still there six days later when the sea begins to subside from back-to-back storms. The wind has pulled into the north, blowing cold, freezing rime ice on the pilings of the docks at Montauk where the draggers come in from the open ocean listing with the weight of salt ice on their rigging — ice that swells a cable to the size of a man's thigh, ice that gathers in the spray from every breaking wave.

Peter and I can see the ice forming in fragile, pale rings just above the blades of our oars, marking the waterline of our strokes as we finish this December day of fishing. It is our third set and we have five small bass, one of them blind, to show for the first two.

"Getting near the end of the season when them blind bass show up," Ted says when the fish is picked out of the bunt. I carry it to the truck, wondering how the sightless creature can survive, blind in a dark sea. Its eyes are white, like the bleached clamshells on the beach. They resemble two small french peas that have been overcooked to paleness and the loss of all vitality. White, they are, as white as the ice on our oars, as white as the few flakes of snow that blow from behind the dunes, riding the north wind of winter.

I can sense the season slipping away. Suddenly I lose whatever illusions and hopes were sustaining me. I have spent all the money we have earned; I had hoped for one more bunch of fish, one more haul to get me through Christmas. Now I carry a single, blind bass to the truck and hear Ted talk of the end. I argue against it.

"There has got to be a bunch somewhere," I yell from the dory as we load after the third set — this one a dry haul, empty but for a few small whiting, silver on the sand, their outsize mouths gaping. "Why don't we go way west? Jesus Christ, we've got to do something. Come on, Ted. Let's stop fooling around here on your home beach. We've got the truck that can travel. Why aren't we at Sagaponack, or someplace west where the fish are?" I pull a whiting from the meshes where it has been caught with its teeth tangled in the twine. My jerk rips off its jaw. I throw the mangled fish at Ted, who is standing on the beach, hanking the net to make it easier for us to load.

The whiting thumps Ted's waders at the center of his chest. Peter, loading the corks in the dory with me, stops still. Jim, helping Ted, drops his side of the net, looks at me. Ted lifts his eyes, and in them I see a hurt that shatters me. I am chagrined, embarrassed, but most of all, surprised and ashamed. Ted's blue eyes are watery from the cold wind, but there is enough hurt in them for me to believe he weeps.

Peter and Jim are startled, incredulous that I should so affront the acknowledged captain of our crew. I am riven with shame and angry with myself for not recognizing that indeed we have become a crew, that Ted does respect me, has confidence in me, and now has been shaken by this evidence of my instability, my own lack of caring, my own apparent cynicism toward our fellowship. No Posey would have thrown that whiting. I have put myself outside the clan, outside the common understandings of the community, outside the mutual respect of the crew. And, because I have acted with such meanness, such immaturity, such a lack of understanding of our relationship, such ignorance of my place on his crew and such insensitivity to the generosity it took for him to put me there, Ted is hurt and vastly disappointed.

I see, in Ted's full eyes, something I had been blind to all along. I have been accepted. I have been, in the Poseys' eyes, a fisherman — something I never thought I could become, and something I felt certain the Poseys would never acknowledge. But it was never difficult for them. They were ready all along; I had only to do the work, to row, to pull, to grunt, to risk, to stay. For them, that was enough. I was not so gracious. I believed the white chimneys were with me always, their shadows reaching the length of the beach, no matter where we fished.

It was from the house on the dunes that I hurled the whiting at Ted, not from the dory. And, in his eyes after he has been struck by it, I learn that I am the only one who can still see that house. Others see me as a fisherman, and in this snotty disrespect to my captain, I have tainted fishing tradition. I have despoiled Ted's true affection, shamed Jim and Peter, and I discover for myself that I have jeopardized a caring relationship that I have always yearned for, but failed to recognize when it at last entered my life.

"Johnny." That is Ted's only word. Then again, "Johnny." His hand rubs away the blood and gurry from his waders. He shakes his head, no, no, no, but his eyes stay with me.

At last, I find words. "I'm sorry, Ted. I'm sorry. I mean it. I didn't think. I just threw it, without thinking." I lean over the rail of the dory, closer to Ted. I tell myself it is the wind, and not tears in his eyes.

"Ted, it's the fishing. You know how excited I get. I go kind of crazy when I think we may be missing a bunch. You know that.

"I shouldn't have thrown that whiting. I know that. Everybody knows that. It was a stupid trick." I think as I talk that words won't do much, but I don't know any other way. I am so unprepared for the dimensions of my deed I am confused as to how to set things to rights.

For a while, Ted says nothing. He just keeps looking at me, trying to persuade himself, I suppose, that I am truly as dense as I have shown myself to be. He must convince himself to believe that, to understand that there is no other explanation. If there is, if he believes that I am insubordinate; challenging, or ignoring, his leadership; spurning, or mocking, his dignity as a man and the captain of the crew — then he will retaliate: punish me with his fists if he loses his temper, or, if he keeps it, banish me from the beach.

I wonder how much longer this stillness can continue. How long can we stand, rooted to this cold beach like figures in a circus act of living statues? Ted is the first to move. He resumes his chore, hanking the seine, tugging at the corks, sliding the entire net along the sand so it will be piled neatly and close to the dory for Peter and me to load. As he works, Ted talks to Jim.

"We'll make one more set, and that's it. One more, but only if we see some sign of fish. I'm not setting again unless there is something to go on. I've had my last dry haul for this year. We'll cruise the beach after we get loaded, and if we see something, we'll put her in. If not, I'm taking this rig back to the yard till spring."

Jim nods. "OK Cap," he says, and goes back to loading. Peter looks at me.

"Whew," he says gently. That's all.

I begin loading the lead line. Part of me wishes I were some-

where else; another, larger, part is in turmoil. I churn with the comprehensions that my thoughtless move has triggered, and I wonder if Ted will ever understand how much I regret throwing that fish, or realize how much I have discovered as a result of it. The reality that we are moving again, that routine is restored, gives me hope that the relationships I have wounded — and recognized at one and the same moment — can somehow be made whole.

I stare out to sea, at the far horizon. Inshore, the ocean is calmed by the wind off the land. The waves are sharp, curling, and the northerly gale blows mare's tails of spume off the crests as they move toward the beach. But on the far horizon, where the wind reaches beyond the lee, the seas build and cut a jagged pattern along the line where water meets the sky. I try to preoccupy my thoughts with the oddness of the seascape created by the wind offshore. The horizon jumps, vibrates, and I watch it, imagining what it must be like out there in a small boat bucking the chop and the freezing spray.

Dark clouds roll like cannonballs across the sky; they are the leading edge of a cold front, sweeping down from the north, pushing winter before it. More fat flakes of snow slant across the dunes, the sand hisses against the side of the dory; I can feel the twine stiffening in my hands as the windchill freezes the sea-soaked netting where it lies on the beach. In the afternoon light of the short day, the seawater turns green, splotched white with its offshore waves — a white made starker by the gunmetal sky and the hurtling snow.

I wonder to myself if what I see can be birds, or a snow patch, whirling in its own tight orbit far beyond the bar. In the snow it is difficult to tell. Then, as they move closer, the birds emerge, tossing and turning in a white cluster like the snowflakes, but with a focus to their churning. They are edging, bit by bit, toward the shore, and as they come nearer I can see white water at the bottom of their funnel-shaped flock. They are gulls and gannets, and they are working over fish. There can be no doubt now about that. This is a sure sign, the finest kind of sign.

"Hey, look there! Look there!" I yell. I find a freedom in the rush, a setting to rights in the fact of the birds. It is a signal that fish are there as certain as any I could have spotted. Ted looks, and he yells too.

"That's a bunch, that's sure. That's a bunch. Looks like they're moving inshore too." He begins trotting to the truck, his waders thumping as he moves. "Come on, boys. Come on, get that twine in the dory. Jesus, Johnny, get moving, will you."

Peter whoops and grins. Together we hustle in the last of the seine. Ted starts the truck, pulls the rig along the beach a bit, closer to the fish. They are still too far offshore to be reached, but they are on top, moving in.

Their activity is frantic. The green sea is frothed with constant splashing. I see geysers of breaking water spout aloft, to be atomized by the wind. I have never seen such large gouts of foam in a school of bass before. These are, I decide, either very large bass, or else the school is feeding on a different sort of cold water bait. There is an aura of panic to the scene that I have never before witnessed.

"Something is driving those bass," Ted yells. He is standing on top of the truck cab, looking out to sea. "Them fish ain't feeding. Something is feeding on them." Ted takes off his long-billed cap. His silver-white hair, close-cropped, stands out against his tanned face. He holds his arm with the cap in his hand to shield his eyes from the wind and snow. "Them's porpoise, that's what they are. That's what's going on out there. Them porpoise are driving those bass. God dammit, there's no telling what will happen, goddamn porpoise."

I can see them now — black fins rising from curved black backs, sliding from under the green sea, sleek, surging, pushing aside the water in wedged welts of white foam. And in front of the wedges, the bass scatter, flashing, panicking like minnows before the assault of the torpedoing scores of porpoise. I am stunned by the scale of the slaughter. There must be a hundred or more porpoise, a vast school. Like wolves running down a pack of lambs, they are herding the small bass, this way, then that way, but always toward the beach where the stripers will have to leap to the sand if they are to find sanctuary from these predators.

The entire mass, hunters and hunted, moves into the surf line. We can hear the splashing now. We can hear the explosive whoosh of air from the porpoise blow-holes when they surface. The bass are practically at our feet. The regular pattern of the waves is set asunder by the turmoil at the ocean's edge. The porpoise look huge to me — great black hulks, roaring like locomotives along the walls of the waves.

One breaches in the wash. His entire twelve-foot length comes free of the surf in a great leap that takes the creature from its element, from the green and white sea, and pinions it against the cannonball clouds of this winter sky. The porpoise underside is ivory white, a curving bib beneath its jaws. And there, caught across those jaws is a striped bass at the moment of its doom. The porpoise teeth close. Incredibly, the creature is still aloft against my horizon like a demon come alive. Bright bass blood spills along the ivory bib, red against the cream.

The porpoise falls back into the sea; foam fountains against the skyline; the porpoise and its fellows are once again curving black backs beneath the waves. The leaping creature no longer hangs against the sky, yet hangs forever in my memory.

The school of bass turns offshore now. Having found no sanctuary in the surf, the frenzied fish once again make for deeper water — anything to get shed of their tormentors. I can see that we, too, are doomed.

"They're getting away. They're moving out." I am desperate. "Ted, Ted, come on, let's set, let's go."

"No, Johnny, no." Ted shakes his head. Like me, he must be wondering what stars have crossed this day. "We can't set around them porpoise. They'll tear the seine to shreds. Besides, the bass are moving too fast. They'll never sit still long enough for us to set around them, not being chased like that." Ted watches as the patch of white water, the black backs and the funnel of birds moves southwest, across the outer bar. "We might as well give it up. Porpoise moving along the beach like that, there ain't going to be a bass inshore between here and Shinnecock."

So this is how a season ends, with the four of us, sitting on the dory, or in the truck, watching as the last school we'll see till spring is pursued by the marauders who have stolen what was to be our Christmas haul, the twenty boxes of money fish that would have put cash in my pockets, paid some of my bills.

Snow comes harder now, blowing flat, straight across the beach. The wind is picking up; I can hear the sand hissing more steadily against the dory's windward side. The sky has grown blacker, the sea green, feathered with building whitecaps. The working birds are as difficult to distinguish from the snow as they were when I first saw them, when this entire melodrama began. God damn, why, why couldn't we have had just one break, just this one haul?

Ted climbs into the seat of the big, silver truck, looks down at the chest of his waders where there is still a smear of blood from my thrown whiting, echoing the stain I can see still on the bib of the porpoise.

"Let's go home," Ted says. "Let's go home." He looks at me as I climb down from the dory and walk to the "A" to ride in with Jim. "I'm sorry, Johnny," Ted says as he starts the truck, then calls over the engine roar, "I'm sorry we didn't get that bunch."

I get in the seat with Jim in the "A" with its top still bent from the tree I dropped on it. The snow cuts through the opening, and I wish once again that I hadn't been so dumb. I can't seem to make a move without doing damage.

We head east, along the beach, toward the Amagansett Beach Club. Jim squints and then points from behind the windshield toward Montauk. Leaning out the open window, I see a white-hulled boat rigged for sportsfishing moving along just behind the surf, traveling in the lee of the land.

"What the hell is he doing out there?" I ask.

"Going south, Cap, going south. That's a Montauk charter boat, probably make it to Shinnecock today, Sandy Hook tomorrow, and then down the inland waterway to Florida. Going south, just like those bass." Jim stops the "A," leans out his window for a better look. "That looks like George's boat. It's either him, or Carl. They're always the last to go."

He gets back in the car, turns to look at me with those steady, blue eyes. "That's what I think I'll do someday, Cap," he tells me. "Think I'll go south myself some winter, get a job mating on one of those."

We turn off the beach, on the road home.

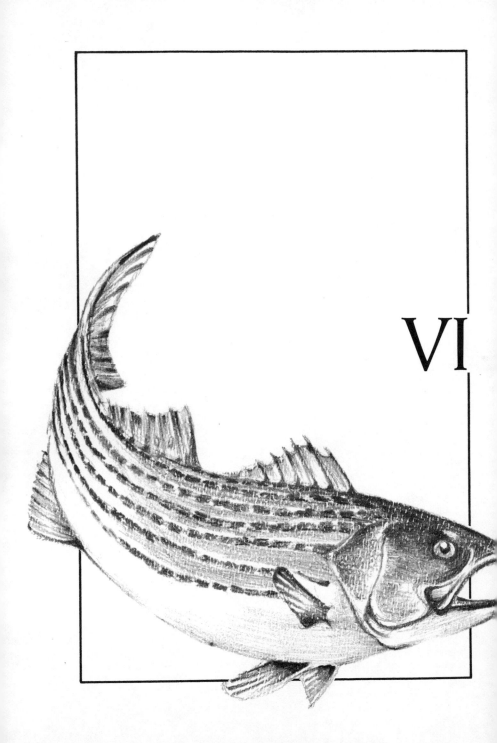

VI

In 1926, flush with money and dreams that had bloomed with his creation of Miami from a Florida swamp, Carl Fisher came to the East End, to Montauk, Long Island's outermost tip, convinced he could work yet another of his transformations on that gnarled and windswept bony finger of land that points to the open Atlantic like an ancient oracle beckoning toward the center of mystery.

Before the crash of '29 shattered his life, his speculation and his dreams, Fisher had ordered a channel dredged across the thin strip of beach that separated Long Island Sound from Montauk Lake — a landlocked body of fresh water just a few hundred yards from the sound. Once the channel was stabilized with a breakwater, Montauk Lake became one of the finest small-boat harbors on the northeast coast. It is still the only harbor within a thirty-minute boat ride of the Point, that meeting place of sound and sea, a surging and turbulent collision of perpetual tides that is the finest inshore saltwater fishing environment between New Jersey and Maine — a coastal strip that is home for nearly forty million Americans.

Four years after Fisher's dredge had made its first cut across the sand, the Union News Dock was built just a few hundred feet from the entrance to the new harbor. Two men, John Messbauer and Gus Pitts, took their commercial fishing skiffs to that dock and converted them to the first charter boats eastern Long Island had known. From that genesis (the seat Gus provided for his early charter clients was a plank lashed from gunwale to gunwale) the Montauk charter boat fleet has grown to include more than one hundred deluxe sportsfishing craft, valued collectively at more than a million dollars. Gus and his two first cousins, Ralph and Clancy Pitts, have been skippering their charter boats out of Montauk for a combined 110 years of fish hunts that has produced catch totals beyond the reasoning of most ordinary fishermen.

Consider the arithmetic. For their cumulative 110 years off Montauk, fishing each year from mid-May to late November, the Pittses have boated an average fifty fish a day for their clients. When they first started, they fished three separate charters a day; now they fish two, and their seasons are booked solidly months, even years, in advance. But allowing for missed days, even some bad days, Pitts boats have brought some two million fish into the Montauk dock since 1931.

Of those fish, striped bass and bluefish account for the large majority. The striper has always been Gus's primary trophy; his development of inshore fishing techniques for bass has made him something of a legend along the East Coast. Ralph is considered a more versatile captain; he has caught blue marlin off Eleuthera as well as stripers off Caswell's. And Clancy, like his cousin Gus, stayed inshore, worked the Point, and counted on the striper to fill his fish box and keep the customers returning, season after season. At the current rate of $150 a trip (plus a tip for the mate), at two trips a day for 180 days, Gus, Clancy and Ralph have been grossing about $54,000 apiece for some seven months of work.

Ralph, the last of the Pittses to charter regularly, retired at the close of the 1977 season, leaving Montauk's fleet without a Pitts at the helm for the first time since 1931. The clan left its mark on the development of inshore charter boat fishing; the family skippers cut patterns that are still being followed. With the striper as the focus of their endeavors as guides and fish finders, the Pittses built three strong families and three fine and prosperous businesses.

In Montauk, those patterns are followed, although not always successfully emulated, by one hundred other charter skippers who moor their sleek and powerful boats at the dozen or more docks that now line the shores of Montauk Lake's northern end like spokes from a wheel hub.

Yet, alongside the docks that sprout in other harbors from Key Largo, Florida, to Boothbay Harbor, Maine, the facilities at Montauk Lake are one tree in a forest of pilings that surrounds a recreational fishing fleet that is larger, more costly, more energy consuming, more lavishly equipped with electronic navigational and fish-finding aids than any other, anywhere in the world. Indeed, the East Coast recreational fishing fleet is larger and worth more dollars than the combined working and defense fleets of all but a handful of nations.

From Cape May, New Jersey, to the oily harbor at Portland, Maine, it is the striped bass that lures most of the charter boats. In some inshore waters, like those off Martha's Vineyard, Nantucket, Cuttyhunk and New Bedford, the bass is always the primary fish. Only when the thrashing schools of bluefish arrive on one of their unpredictable journeys, or when the giant tuna cruise by in midsummer, will much of the Massachusetts charter fleet turn away from its daily search for stripers.

There are thousands of vessels out there on any given day between May and November, there close to the heaving border of white waters that embroider the joining of land and sea. As Gus Pitts first discovered in his boat *Marie* before a charter boat fleet existed, striped bass like the surge of the surf, the turmoil of tides in the rocks. Experienced charter boat skippers learn where the fish can be found, and there they return with their clients, day

after day, week after week, month after month, year after year, to find and hook the fish for their parties, who then "catch" their trophy by turning the crank on the reel while the mate stands alongside and gives instructions.

More than three million U.S. anglers a year hire boats to take them fishing, and the largest of the for-hire fleets docks along the northeast coast. There are hundreds of millions of dollars involved in the leisure-time, recreational phenomenon that didn't exist as an industry when Gus Pitts first moored his skiff at the Union News Dock in Montauk Lake. Men like Ernest Hemingway,

S. Kip Farrington, Jr., Mike Lerner, Alfred Glasell, Zane Grey, and New York's Prohibition mayor, Jimmy Walker, were the first big-game fishermen.

With linen line, cane rods, reels with only a leather patch pushed by the thumb to act as a brake, these men and their friends generated a certain macho mystique about saltwater fishing. Then came Philip Wylie with his *Saturday Evening Post* stories about the charter boat pair, Crunch and Des. And after that, after World War II, came a boat-building boom, ship-to-shore radio, radar, loran, depth finders, white-line recorders that can locate a school of fish twenty-five fathoms down, stainless steel and aluminum fighting chairs, tuna towers, flying gaffs, fully stocked floating bars, and televised beer commercials showing Joe America hooked on to a leaping marlin which is rising like a scimitar from the sea over the curve of a charter boat's teakwood transom.

Adventure with a kind of class has become available to anyone with the money. Assembly line workers from Long Island City pool their resources, six of them combining to charter Ralph Pitts and his boat, the *Margaret V*, and his mate Ted Sigler and his two-score rods and reels and a half century of experience off Montauk. Throw a case of beer onto the deck, drop into the fishing chairs and wait for the bass to be found, six guys off the air wrenches looking for what Hemingway said he discovered, what Zane Grey wrote books about. A fantasy come true, for $150 plus a tip for the mate. And how vast the bitterness if the fish don't cooperate. How consuming the anger if the stripers are not to be found. Fantasies without the fish are not enough, not for 150 bucks for a lousy few hours.

So Ralph and his counterparts learn to find the fish, not just some days, but every day. No ruined fantasies, no end to the business. The bass and bluefish get tossed on the docks like so much cordwood, the decks are swept of crumpled beer cans and gurry, the boat is hosed down, ready for the afternoon party. Thump and thump and thump, more bass go on the dock as the day ends, and

Ralph gets home early so he can be up the next morning at four, up to take a couple from Rahway in the morning, a group of businessmen from Mattapan in the afternoon. There is no end to the Americans who want half a day in a dream boat, who want to feel the rod bend and jerk in their hands while the reel sings with strain and the forty-two-pound striped bass fights and tugs for his life at the end of the line and the Montauk Light looks down on four hundred pleasure and charter boats crisscrossing the blue waters with their white hulls like so many drops of milk on a Dresden plate.

The place has become so crowded with boats that as the charter fleet heads for home at sunset, another smaller fleet starts out. These are the fishermen who fish through the night rather than struggle with the crush of marine traffic under the light where each boat sweeps three lines, 150 feet apiece, through the tide-churned waters where bass and bluefish swim.

It is a sight Carl Fisher must have dreamed of.

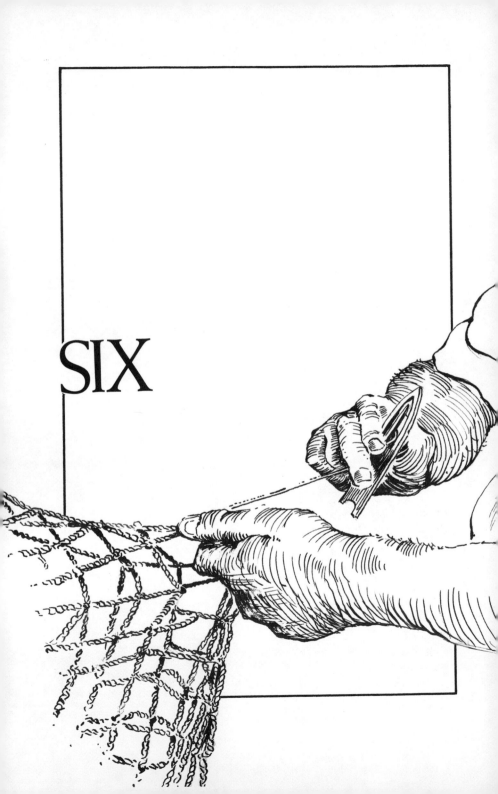

SIX

No sooner do the porpoises end our fishing for the year, than Ted starts talking about the trip to Albany. I can't take him as seriously on the topic as he apparently likes to be taken. I mean, it seems preposterous to me that surfcasters and charter boat skippers, who catch most of the bass anyway, would work to put a handful of haul seiners out of business. It's a move against one family, really. If the Posey clan quit seining, there would be but one or two crews left on the entire East End.

For Ted, the threat is not only real, but his sole off-season preoccupation is fighting it. He shouts at me about it as we pull the long seine into the loft of his fish house where the twine will stay clean and dry until April when the fishing starts again.

"Gawd dammit Johnny, don't just stand there and say you don't see how those fellas in Albany can put us out of business. They done it in other states up and down the coast." Ted puts down the cork line and walks across the net to me. He holds his left hand out like a board, and points at it with the index finger of his right, as if the thick, battered block of flesh with its cracked and callused palm is a checklist totaling every indignity and injustice the enemies of haul seining have ever inflicted on the Poseys' primary occupation.

He taps the left palm, just at the base of the little finger. "There's Massachusetts. Hardly a fit place to haul a seine there, but what there is has been put off limits. Can't use a net of any kind. Them fish just lay in the rocks there by the thousands, and the charter boats and casters pick away at them all day and all night. Just look at the landings from Massachusetts if you want to know how many bass those fellas are shipping. Half of them are in it for the money, just like us. They want it all, I suppose. Can't give the commercial man a fair shake, can't let us get our fair share."

His voice is louder now, his face inches from mine as I lean further back, trying to ease Ted's blast. His index finger moves another notch on his own, leathery checklist. "Then there's Connecticut. Took the fisherman's living right away from him, down there, they did.

"Well, they ain't going to do it in New York, no they ain't, not if we stick together, get up there to Albany and speak our piece. Ain't that right, Johnny? We kept that law out of the assembly for five years now, and we'll do it again this year if I can get these fellas off their ass and get them up there. Don't look good if we don't have a crowd up there. The politicians think we don't care if we don't show up. You're coming with me ain't you Johnny?" He pokes his finger at my chest this time.

"Sure Ted, if you say so. I'd like to make the trip anyway. It's just that I can't believe those guys would try to put you out of business."

"Well, now, there's a lot you don't know, ain't there Johnny?" Ted looks at me, reconsiders, then adds a tenderizer as he turns back to the corks. "There's a lot none of us knows, now that's for certain."

I think about those words often during the following weeks while I'm painting walls, doors, windows and trim in the huge, cold, summer places on Lily Pond Lane. Jim and Peter and I have landed a pair of contracts to give two mansions a new coat of paint and a tidying while the owners spend the winter in the city. It seems like an ideal job to me, which is one reason that we are able to do it for such low wages. Here we are, inside for the most part, out of the weather, but still together, working on our own time at a job that will be done just as it's time to get back fishing again.

Painting is mostly a common-sense operation, and we have done enough of it on boats and gear to understand the basics, like scraping, patching, mixing, and puttying. We stand, slapping full brushes against the plaster walls, looking out the windows across the dunes to the freezing sea that undulates and heaves at the beach. As I daydream, I can see the bass at Ditch Plain, I can see the porpoise on that last day, and I can relive the torment of the moment when I hurled the whiting at Ted. Which is why I cling so to the elements of forgiveness in his talk about Albany. He is not, I believe, a grudge-holding man. As the days pass, I begin to believe I can be back on the beach with Ted in the spring, and that makes the painting go more easily.

Jim and Peter make it go more easily too. Banter and music from the radio move from room to room as we do, and there is the sense of fellowship that flows from the rather bizarre nature of our mutual environment. There are probably forty houses on Lily Pond Lane, and every one of them is enormous. They are great, rambling collections of rooms, sun porches, stairways, closets, shingled turrets and towers that rise like so many summer castles at the rim of the Atlantic. The driveways are long, awash in crunching gravel and bluestone; the vast lawns are peopled with clipped hedges, some cut in the shapes of oversized birds, benches and leaping whales. Garages and barns and servants' quarters are scattered around the mansions like so many courtiers kneeling before their monarchs, and inside the chill rooms of the main houses full-length portraits stare down from the walls, crystal gleams in the cabinets and porcelain lamps stand alone atop Louis XV tables. Yet, in the entire procession of palaces that marches up the ocean-side road, there is no one. In all the great houses, in all the hundreds of rooms with their linen spreads on the beds and the fragrance of salt air trapped in the wicker furniture of summer, in all these spaces there are no other humans but the three of us, moving like voyagers from a time warp across interiors that are part of another history.

In the echoing footsteps of our collective solitude, we are drawn closer. We become the mutual proprietors of the places we are painting; we enter these separate worlds each morning, free of fishing's demands, and instead become a part of summers past, alone in an opulent isolation that is far from our present reality, and yet so much a part of our own histories that we are like children on a picnic who wander into an empty house of candy, discovered deep in the woods.

We are playing. And as we play at painting — doing a job that professional painters consider work — we talk about fishing, we talk about our lives, and we talk about our dreams for our futures. But there is no thought articulated in these fanciful places that is not touched with a kind of illusion, as if we are children wearing grown-up clothes. It is as if Smiley's drowning were make-believe, as if the dismal end of the season never happened, as if each of us has no serious doubts about whether he can survive as a fisherman, or has begun to question whether he will find his dreams on the beach and in the sea. Anxieties somehow vanish in these rooms with their portraits on the walls and crystal goblets in the butler's pantry. Even if we try — and we seldom do — we can not see these houses merely for what they are: the overstated summer homes of the very rich. In our aloneness within these chill and silent estates, we transform them into a stage for our own flights of fancy — a stage we leave each evening at dusk, smelling of turpentine and putty as we head home to the reality of our empty wallets.

The winter spins by on the pivot of our painting, and our games are interrupted only once — when Ted calls to tell us the bill to outlaw seining striped bass will have its hearing the next day in Albany.

"Be down to my house at four," he says, yelling into the phone as usual, giving us orders as if we are going fishing instead of packing into Ted's big Buick for a trip up the thruway. "That will give us five hours to get there. Hearing isn't scheduled until ten. I don't think those fellas get to work until nine, but we want to be sure to get there before they do, ain't that right, Johnny?"

We should be going fishing, that's what I feel the next morning when the three of us pile out of the "A" in Ted's yard. He's up. Ted is always up. The light is on over the porch; I can hear the surf rustling and thumping on the beach about a mile away. But we are dressed in our good clothes, not our waders, and we sit stiffly around Ted's kitchen table, drinking instant coffee, putting peanut butter on toast, and trying to get used to the image of Ted with his face shiny-smooth shaven, flushed beneath his silver hair, atop a buttoned, starched shirt collar, plugged with a necktie that divides the smooth, hard lapels of a brown suit that appears to have acquired a metallic rigidity from hanging in Ted's closet for the other 364 days of the year.

Ted is aware of the costume. He speaks directly to the issue. "Look some different, don't I boys? Well, we don't want them politicians up there thinking we're some kind of hicks. We can look just as good as them surfcasters. Better, yes, better." He swallows all of his coffee, even though I can see the steam curling from his cup, takes a bundle of keys from his pocket and gives us our marching orders. "Come on boys, come on. We'll get breakfast when we get there."

Christ, I think, this man is never at rest. We'll have to wait five hours now before we eat, maybe more. Ted sees the legislators in Albany the same way he sees the bass — they can be caught if you start early enough.

We pile into the Buick, Ted drops it into gear and roars out of the yard, flicking bits of clamshell with his spinning tires as he goes. The sun doesn't begin to show until we reach the Throgs Neck Bridge at the other end of the island, and, until we get to

Albany, we stop only for toll booths. We have come nearly three hundred miles, and Albany is just waking up.

"Boys, I gotta piss something fierce," says Ted, pulling into a gas station.

"Us likewise, Cap," Jim replies, and we pile out. I am not prepared for such a grimy city. I have thought of the state capital as a clean place, at least, but it is a gray and dingy one. Not even the dome of the capitol building on the horizon can take the gritty edge off Albany's gloomy presence. It is a deep winter morning; old snow foams dirty at the curbs; the gray sky and the gray streets make for a cheerless day. Ted is not bothered. He has been here before and he concentrates on following his plan, shepherding us back into the car, giving orders once again.

"Let's go, let's go. We'll get right over there and find out where we're supposed to go, get the lay of the land, don't you know."

It proves a tough land to get the lay of. Like a tour party, we follow Ted as he trots up and down the halls, looking here, looking there. The place is a maze to me, smelling of tobacco and disinfectant — a cross between Penn Station and a men's club. Doors open and close, men in dark suits smoke cigars and walk by. Ted can not learn what room the bass bill will be heard in. He stops a man walking the hall.

"Tell me," he yells, "where can I find out where this bass bill will get its airing?"

"Right down there," the man points, "at the clerk's office." He starts to walk off, then turns back. "I think that hearing has been postponed, but you better check."

Ted's voice fills the corridor. "Postponed. Postponed, after we drove all the way here." He stumps down the hall. "Postponed. That's bullshit."

We watch and wait as Ted leans over the half door at the clerk's office. We can hear the Posey voice start loud, then grow less and less emphatic, until we can hear nothing. Ted comes back after considerable (for him) soft conversation. He comes close to us, and talks even more softly, in almost a conspiratorial whisper.

"Something's going on here. Something funny. I know that bill was to come up today. The Baymen's Association man here told me. Nick called me yesterday. He knows what he's doing." Ted bangs his fist into his palm. "Those pinhookers, they're up to something. Well, they ain't going to fool me. We're going to stay right here until we learn what they're up to. They're a sly bunch, they are. Probably want us to think there ain't no hearing, then they'll have it all to themselves." He turns and starts walking out of the building, watching for us to follow.

"Come on, come on boys. We'll get us a hotel room and hang right in here till we figure this out."

We do get the hotel room, just one, for the four of us. It never crosses Ted's mind that the place may be small quarters for four men. He thinks it foolish to hire any more space.

Ted waves his arm around. "There's plenty of room here. Pull those mattresses off the beds for two of us, the other two can sleep on the box springs. No need of spending good money for one night in this town. Charge you an arm and a leg for it, anyway."

He goes over and looks out the window at the grimy sky. "Ain't much of a day for being out. You fellas stay here while I go over and try to find out what's going on. I'll find Nick, he'll know if the hearing is postponed, or what. Stay here until I call you."

We stay, and we wait. We lie around, watching television, going down to the lobby for a snack. We nap on the beds, and we wonder where Ted is, what he's doing, and we ask why he hasn't called. It is after dark before the door opens and Ted comes in. He has someone with him, a stranger, a man in a blue suit we have never seen before. He's a middle-aged, dark-browed man, and he flashes a big smile at us as he walks in. Ted closes the door and begins talking to us in his quiet, conspiratorial tone.

"Now you fellows listen carefully. I think I've got this worked out. Now Mr. Santo is a New York legislator. He tells me that he can get the bass bill killed. 'Course, he'll have to do some extra work, it will take a good deal of his time." Ted looks at each of us, his blue eyes narrow; he is expectant, waiting, but none of us knows what for.

"Well, you know what I mean, don't you Jim?" Ted nudges Jim's ribs. Still no response. Ted bulls ahead. "Well, what I mean is, it will cost maybe three hundred dollars in fees and stuff. Now that ain't much when you consider, what's at stake here." Ted puts his hand on the stranger's shoulder, "And we know this fella can do the job." The man smiles again; Ted keeps talking. "Well, I just ain't got that much money with me. I can go two hundred, that's about it. I was hoping you boys could come up with the rest. This fella says we got to get this done tonight, or it may be too late."

Jim and Peter and I understand now. Ted wants money. This is, in fact, a kind of bribe. Jim objects. "I don't know, Ted. How can we be sure? I mean, what else did you learn today? I'd like to know more about this first."

It is awkward, talking like this while the stranger stands there, listening. None of us is sure just what to do. We don't want to embarrass Ted, but we don't have that much money, and what we do have has come hard.

The arguments fly; Ted's face gets redder. Jim is tight as a tick anyway; I can't see him parting with any money for any reason, and he certainly isn't likely to give it to a man he doesn't know for a service he doesn't understand. I don't have much more than twenty dollars in my pocket, so the argument is decided as far as I'm concerned. Peter wants to do right by Ted, but I can tell that the talk thus far hasn't persuaded Peter to give up any of the cash he has worked so hard to earn.

The politician evidently senses he has not met with a totally enthusiastic reception. He feels uneasy, I think, standing there listening to Jim make statements like, "How do we know he'll do what he says he'll do?" After a while, the stranger makes it easier for all of us by announcing that he's leaving. "I've got to get back for a meeting," he explains as he opens the door. "I'll call back in an hour or so and see what you've decided."

Ted is angry; Jim is stubborn, as always. They go at it for almost half an hour, both of them getting more and more flushed. Jim's face is crimson under his black hair, his blue eyes flash and his jaw is set. Ted, at last, gives in.

"It's your money, boys. You do what you want with it. I can't force you. But you don't know how things work up here, is all. We may have wasted this whole trip." He puts his hand on Jim's shoulder. "But no hard feelings. Let's go out and get a drink and some food. We'll feel better after that. What do you say, Jim? How does that strike you?"

"That sounds good to me, Cap, sounds good to me." Jim starts pulling on the heavy wool shirt that doubles as his outer jacket and the four of us head out to look for a place to eat. We end up in a bar-restaurant that also has a strip act of sorts. We drink too much beer. Ted keeps telling us the stripper is lovely, but she must be about forty, and she's fat. With Ted telling us all the way back about how horny the steak made him we finally get to the room. Ted and Peter sleep on the floor mattresses, Jim and I take what's left of the beds, and I spend most of the night trying to sleep through Ted's snoring. It's the loudest I've ever heard.

The phone rings in the morning before we are fully awake. It's for Ted. We listen to his end of the talk. "Yes, Nick. . . . Is that so? . . . Well now, ain't that fine. . . . You did a good job Nick. . . . No, we'll be leaving as soon as we get collected here. . . . Yup, goodbye." Ted hangs up and looks at each of us. "That was Nick. He says the reason there wasn't a hearing yesterday is that Perry Duryea killed the bill in committee. It's never even going to come to the floor. Looks like we're OK for this year, boys."

"Did Nick say what time he got the news?" Jim asks.

Ted thinks a moment. "He said Perry called him yesterday

afternoon, but Nick couldn't get away to call us till later. We must have gone out for supper by then."

"Then that politician you brought up here could have known the bill was dead before he got here, couldn't he?" asks Jim. "He could have been trying to get our money for a job that Perry had already done. How do you like that? Now that's a politician for you."

Ted understands. He shakes his head from side to side. "Well, I never. Now that's a kick in the head. Jesus Christ, Jim, I'm some glad we didn't give him that money. Well, well, well. That son of a bitch tried to skin us for three hundred dollars. What do you think of that." Ted pulls on his shirt, but doesn't add the tie this time. "Come on boys," he says, "let's go home."

And that's our trip to Albany. The haul seiners are safe for another year. The three of us, Jim and Peter and I, laugh about Ted while we're painting. For the rest of the winter, we joke about the stripper and tell each other how happy we are we didn't get fleeced by a crooked pol.

One sunny day during the last week in March, Peter and I are out on a south-facing porch, painting the railing and the white columns. We hear geese flying over and run out on to the lawn to look for the birds. They're almost overhead, flying in a long, wavering wedge with the southwest wind at their tails. They talk and call, and the flock flutters, breaks its formation as the geese become windblown leaves, circling over the pond that's just a short distance from where we're working. Peter knows where the geese are headed.

"John, they're going down in Hook Pond, that's where they are." Peter waves his arm, pointing to the east. "We'll be hearing them most every day now." He breaks into a grin. "You know, John, when those geese start moving, the bass can't be far behind. We'll be into them soon, Cap. We'll be into them soon."

And we are. By April, we quit painting. Peter and I are back on Ted's crew, getting gear ready, looking forward to the first sign of fish, anticipating a first set any day we get good weather after the middle of the month. But Jim isn't with us. Not this time. He has made his decision to try fishing alone. He's had some money put aside all this time, and he shows up on our last day of painting in a new, four-wheel-drive Land Rover.

"This is it," he says, "this is my crew. I can pull the *Peril* with this, winch in a small seine. Between that and my gill nets, I can do just fine. Two boxes for me is like ten boxes on Ted's crew. I ought to be able to catch two boxes a day with this gear, shouldn't I?" He looks at me. Jim has this way of staring. His blue eyes fasten on me, he doesn't talk, he just looks. I don't know anyone else who has this silent directness. Sometimes, when Jim looks at me this way, I don't know how to respond. This is one of those times. I mumble.

"I don't know, Jim. Sure, Cap. I mean, if it doesn't work, we can try something else. Well, we'll be here, anyway. We'll see you on the beach, maybe when you bring your fish into Ted's. We'll see you then."

I have a difficult time acknowledging Jim's departure. We have been together almost every day since that October dawn when we drove together in the dark to the Main Beach to help Swede lift his gill net — the day I first put my hand on twine, pulled my first striper from a net, the day I first decided to try being a fisherman. Jim has been with me for more than a year since that day, at my side, fishing, making nets, cutting wood, drinking, painting, packing fish, eating breakfast ... watching Smiley drown, going under ourselves, in the *Peril*. Jim has been there with me for all that, a presence at my side — a stronger presence, I've always known that. Now he tells me he's going to try fishing solo, by himself, on his own, and I'm not as concerned about whether he can make it as I am worried about whether I'll hold up without Jim.

But I don't say anything like that. I look back at him hoping he can hear the unsaid words, and I say, "We'll see you, then."

But we don't see him that much. Alex joins up with me and Peter on Ted's crew and we work to the west, hoping to meet the bass as they move up the coast from the Chesapeake and the Hudson. Jim says they don't come like drivers on a highway. He theorizes that the fish swing inshore and then offshore as they travel a looping route. "They're just as likely to be off Hither Hills as they are off Sagaponack," he argues, and while we work through April and early May around Georgica and Wainscott, Jim has his gear near Montauk, sets his gill nets off the small beaches and hauls his one-man seine off Napeague and places like that.

It's a strange season. By mid-May we have a few decent hauls on the books, but nothing special — six boxes here, eleven there, then two or three days with nothing. We work our way through the dogfish migration; one morning we can scarcely haul back the net, there are so many dogfish gilled and twisted in the meshes. Ted says we should save some. "Them Chinamen like those doggies," he says, so we ship a few boxes to the Fulton Market. While I wash the fish in Ted's tub, one pregnant dog gives birth. About fifteen miniature replicas of her streamlined, shark-like form start swimming around in the wooden tub, still trailing yolks from their tiny stomachs. I don't want to look at them after the water is drained away and they flop around on the sand and gurry.

After the dogs come the horseshoe crabs, the blowfish and the menhaden. We get huge netfuls of them. Ted doesn't mind; any fish are money to him. But I want bass. Blowfish just lie there puffing and grunting in the net; it's a day's work to skin them for the market. Menhaden quiver and flip; we let most of them go. And the horseshoe crabs get their ancient shapes tangled in the twine; they twist their barbed tails through the meshes. We end up throwing them high on the beach, on their backs where they stay, their spiked tails and spiny feet poking vainly in the air. After a day of no bass, but all the other trash, I long for the sight of the bronze backs, the long shapes hurtling through the waves, the wakes rising in the wash.

But we go through a week with nothing but blowfish and dog-fish. Even Ted wants a change.

"I heard yesterday they was going to open the Gut at Georg-ica," he tells us after we finish the third set of the morning with nothing to show but three stripers, a half box of dogs and a beach littered with horseshoe crabs. "Why don't we take a run up there, see if that's so? Could be some bass gathered up there."

In the spring, after the snows have melted and the equinoctial rains have gone by, Georgica Pond is so filled that some of it floods the cellars of the summer places built along the perimeter of its marshy shores. Under some pressure from homeowners — many of them rich — the town highway department sends a bulldozer to the Gut, the thin strip of barrier beach that separates one end of the brackish pond from the Atlantic. Once the dozer cuts a narrow furrow across the sand and makes a ditch just deep enough to allow the pond waters some movement, the stream soon becomes a river as the pond waters push the sand aside, forced by the tons of stored water to a velocity that sends the current cascading across the beach to collide with the Atlantic's breaking waves. After a day, the channel is feet deep, the sandy delta extends far into the surf, and the Gut becomes a confused, swirling, meeting place of the two watery masses where waves break at odd angles and the normal ponderous rhythms of the sea become fragmented and unpredictable.

Stripers are exhilarated by the confusion; they congregate in the tumult, drawn by the eons of their beginnings to the scent of fresh water and by the tiny baitfish that are tumbled from their Georgica sanctuary. But the tumult that draws the bass is also their defense against the seiners. Because the sand delta builds so quickly and because the seas become so capricious under the influence of the tumbling flow, the Gut is all but impossible to set. Either the currents make a mass of the seine, shifting sands suck down the lead line, or the angling seas swamp a dory when they catch her broadside.

Ted knows what goes on; he has tried the Gut before. As we stand there on the east bank of the cut across the beach that was not there until yesterday, we can tell the waters have been surging for a full twenty-four hours. The banks are steep, the delta has already built offshore. Ted watches the dark waters of the pond flow past him for a long time before he speaks.

"It's past its peak. By tomorrow, there won't be much more than a trickle coming out of here." He looks toward the sea. "No surf to speak of. Anybody can set this place in the morning. Ding and Frank and Bobby probably all be rushing up here trying to get this set. Be low tide, then. High tide around midnight. That's when we ought to be here. What do you say to that? Want to try setting this place at night?"

I look at Peter; his wide eyes are staring at me. We do the rowing, we're the ones who'll be pulling through waves we can't see. Then Peter laughs, he begins to bubble. "Sure, Cap, sure. Let's do it. I think it's great." He is so captivated by the anticipation of adventure, his innate vitality rushes through him the way the Georgica waters rush through the Gut. He carries me along with him.

Like kids preparing for a camp-out, we go downtown, buy hot dogs and beer, come back to the Gut, build a big fire and lie around it, waiting for the tide, watching for the moon, and listening to the sound of the waves, rolling and hissing in the dusk. My white chimneys are just down the beach. I have spent evenings at the Gut before, evenings when we walked up the beach from that house, laden with picnic gear, my brothers and I and our friends, on our boys' adventures. Peter was here then, and I look across the fire at him, seeing the boy so alive in his grinning face. He and I are still boys and I wonder if we shall ever grow up. Here we are, in our thirties, playing a new game at the Gut, but playing, nonetheless.

But the game has become wilder. It is after midnight when Ted is certain the tide has reached its flood and has turned. The nearly full moon sheds a silver light whenever the low clouds slide past, and the tops of the short seas that build in the southwest breeze glow with phosphorescence. How can we set? If we do not get swamped, I tell myself, it will be sheer luck, ignorance, and more luck. We can only get into our seats, pretend the sea is flat calm, and row as if we were setting off on a procession at high noon, one stroke after the other.

And we do. I can not guess if Ted wishes he had never made the plan. He doesn't let on, merely tells us to get in, shoves with Alex, and then jumps in and starts with his "Pull, boys, pull!" We do pull, but it is a discordant and clumsy stroke that we set in the dark. We can not anticipate the timing or the dimensions of the seas. In the random patterns of the Gut waters, our blindness is made worse. Oars meant to bite the water, splat against the foaming crest of the chop, or dig too deep. The dory rolls, wallows, slaps and shudders.

Beyond us, out on the delta, we can hear the hissing and whooshing of the rollers cresting. How the hell, I wonder, are we going to get through those? Ted has tied a waterproof flashlight to the bunt buoy. I watch and hope for it to go overboard soon. At least then we'll know we are halfway.

Peter is yelling, not saying words, but giving vent to his tension with loud yells that cascade over my head along with the sighing of the wind and the sibilant rushing of the surf. The stars and moon are steady overhead as the dory continues its bucking beneath. Ted grunts steadily as he tosses twine overboard. The bunt goes out. We can't see where it's going, or even if the corks are up. This is a crazy and foolish set. It seems that everywhere I look I see the luminous crests of breaking seas, toppling toward me from the black. There is nothing, absolutely nothing, we can do except row, pretending this is a daylight set, nothing more. We are here inside the wet purse of the Atlantic where it is too dark to see beyond the gunwales and our only guides are in the heavens or there on the sand where the remains of our evening fire glow red on that beach of my memories.

We turn toward the beach just inside the rollers that foam over the bar — great pale green strips on the black ocean, always vanishing just before they reach us. We row with the seas now; the waves are on our stern. Instead of bucking and slapping, the dory slides and slips, moving almost too fast for Ted to unload the seine. I feel my oar thump on the sand and I join Peter's yelling. "We're there, we're there. We're on the beach."

When both oars strike the sand, I turn to look over the bow and try to judge where we are in relation to the beach. Alex is waving his flashlight just a few steps ahead. I jump overboard, the water rises to my waist, spills in the side of my waders, but I can walk, tugging the dory toward Alex. Peter jumps too, joins me. Together we pull the dory and Ted through the last of the wash. He drops the jack as we pull. We have set the entire seine. We have done it in confused waters, in the dark, rowing more by instinct than by any landmarks. We did not swamp, we did not come ashore with half the net in the boat, or leave ourselves stranded with the net gone, too far offshore. By God, we are fishermen.

We get to the business of hauling. We must haul by hand; in the dark, winches are too relentless. They will keep turning even though a finger is caught in the rope, even though twine is being torn by a faulty knot tied in the dark. We can not use machines when we can not see. Pulling by hand it seems to take hours to retrieve Ted's long seine from the sea. But we keep hauling, and soon, in the glow of the truck headlights, we can see bass slicing from quarter to quarter. We are close to each other now; the shortening net pulls us together. We strain, heave, and the bunt begins to show, swollen with fish. We yell back and forth; we know we have a good haul.

The tide is ebbing strongly. We can't pull the bunt any further across the broad reach of wet sand that's exposed as the water falls. Alex starts Ted's big silver truck, moves it toward the bunt, then stops. Ted wants to know why.

"What's wrong Alex? Get that thing down here."

"Don't know, Cap. I think the gears are jammed. Transmission's gone, or something like that."

"Jesus," Ted yells. "Ain't that always the way. What the hell can we do now?"

Alex tinkers with the truck. We can hear tools clattering before he speaks. "Ted, I think I can fix it. Have to wait for daylight, though."

We run a line down to the bunt, stretched like a grain bag around its cargo. The fish are quiet, the tide is ebbing, they aren't going anywhere. It's almost three o'clock. We go back and sit around the fire until four-thirty when the first light shows in the eastern sky.

As the dawn glows and then as the sun rises, Alex works on the truck's gearbox. Cursing quietly most of the time, he is alone

with his mystery. None of us comprehend the principles of a gear-box; we wouldn't know what was wrong if we were looking right at the broken part.

But Alex knows. At five-thirty, after the sun has been up half an hour, he starts the truck, puts a wrench in the open gearbox and engages the gears so the truck moves. As the gears turn, they throw oil, blackening Alex and the truck seats. But the system

works. We get down to the bunt, hitch on, and pull it high enough up the sand so we can unload the fish into the truck and get the dory and the seine on the trailer.

By the time we finish, Alex is bathed in oil. "Some shit, isn't it, John?" he says to me, waving his wrench in protest. "Good thing there's nobody moved into them houses yet." He gestures toward the silhouettes on the dunes. I can see the white chimneys far to the east, catching the rising sun. "They'd think we was crazy down here, up the night through, and soaked in oil, rowing in that ocean at night, just for a few fish." He wipes his eyes with a rag. "We gotta be crazy to do this."

It is almost evening when we finish weighing and boxing the fish. Just as Peter and I are about to leave, Jim pulls up in his Rover, backs up to the door, and tosses about two hundred pounds of medium bass on the floor. He turns on the hose to wash them down, then sees our twenty-one boxes waiting for the truck that will take them to Fulton Market. He looks at me with those blue eyes, that long look, then breaks the silence.

"Got a bunch, did you, Cap?"

"Well, yes, Jim. We got a few. Up at the Gut."

Peter moves to the fish, starts helping Jim toss them into the scale. I go get a box, start shoveling ice. It is almost as if the three of us were back together again. But when we're done, Jim's two boxes look small compared to our twenty-one.

Peter, good Peter, throws his arm around Jim. "You'll get 'em, Cap. You'll get 'em. Just wait. You'll come in here with a bunch one of these days."

Jim is over looking at the box of shipping tags the fish brokers make certain is always full. He studies the tags with that quizzical frown he affects, then he turns to Peter.

"Who did you fellows ship to? I don't want all my fish going to the same man as yours. Between us, we're liable to bring down the price." He smiles, looks at me, then imitates Ted. "Ain't that right, Jawnny? Ain't that right?"

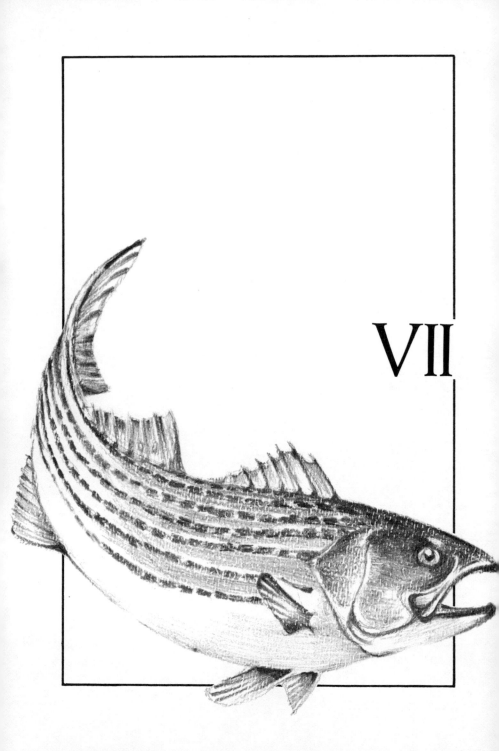

VII

L ike the striped bass, which was sold by colonists to help finance public education a century before the Declaration of Independence, the Fulton Fish Market has beginnings which reach back more than three hundred years. When the first Dutch settlers began building a port in what is now lower Manhattan, they met at a spot on the East River called Smith's Valley, or "Vly" as it was known in the Dutch idiom of the day. The meeting place evolved to become a market where food, fish and goods brought across the Atlantic were sold and traded.

By the mid-1600s, the place was known as the Vly Market, which became the Fly Market, by then official enough to be mentioned in the first water lot grants on the East River, awarded to merchants and brokers in 1686. In 1821, the market became primarily a center for the sale of fresh-caught fish and was renamed Fulton Fish Market, the name it still bears. The strip of land — four small city blocks long, pressed hard against the East River on South Street by lower Manhattan's financial district — is the oldest, busiest fresh fish market in the nation, and the prices set there are the key to the prices paid to commercial fishermen the length of the northeast coast.

There are, however, very few fishermen who can tell you how those prices are set. The process that begins with the arrival of a box of fish or a bushel of clams at midnight, and ends a day or so later when a broker sends the fisherman a check in the mail, is a process as mysterious, as unfathomable, as intricate as any aspect of the national economy. If they do indeed comprehend its mysteries, the twenty-or-so fish brokers, whose small, steel-doored stalls line the market, have never fully explained their formulas.

Some elements of the pricing mix are more comprehensible than others, however. Glut is the most obvious (although one of the least predictable) price killers. When five hundred boxes (about fifty thousand pounds) of medium-sized bluefish shipped in from Long Island meet fifteen hundred boxes sent the same day from New Jersey, the market is overwhelmed. Bluefish are difficult to keep fresh; their enzymes break down the cellular tissue more rapidly than those of almost any other fish. What blues are unsold by the end of a warm June morning on South Street must be dumped. Instead of the money they had counted in their heads as they worked through the night extricating bluefish from their gill nets, the fishermen get a bill from Fulton to cover the costs of shipping the catch by truck from Montauk.

"It don't pay to ship," is the way the commercial men put it when they are aware that the market is overloaded. They count on the "green sheet" as their most dependable source of much important information. The green sheet's proper title is *The Fishery Market News Report,* and it is issued each day Fulton is open by the National Marine Fisheries Service, and mailed to thousands of East Coast fishermen within twenty-four hours after the market closes. It has been printed on sea green sheets of legal-sized paper for decades, thus the "green sheet" identification.

Within the puzzles of its abbreviations (sup lt = supply light ... lmp,mxd,flk = lump, mixed, flake) and its small type, the green sheet hides bushels of information for the fisherman who reads it carefully. Beyond pricing trends, the green sheet reports on where fish are being caught, what trawlers have landed with what loads, and what methods are being used to catch what fish. An impatient striped bass fisherman in Massachusetts, for example, can find daily progress reports in the green sheet of the striper's spring migration. The sheet will record the arrival of Maryland stripers in April, then the first New Jersey fish will be sold at Fulton, a transaction duly noted in the green sheet on the very day of the event. By May, the Massachusetts reader will get more good news from his mailbox: the bass have arrived on eastern Long Island. When that happens, Cape Cod does not have long to wait.

In addition to acting as a daily recorder of fish movements, the green sheet also helps protect both fisherman and middleman by publishing the average prices paid for every single species of fish, shellfish, and crab that moves through Fulton's narrow streets. When a gill netter gets the bad news that his bluefish had to be dumped, he can verify the disaster in the pages of the green sheet. Without it, he might decide he was being cheated and short-changed by a broker — a decision that has led to occasional violence during Fulton's long history.

It is, however, more often misunderstandings and communications failures that lead to arguments between the supplier of fresh fish and their Fulton seller. Several of the market's firms have been doing business for more than a century; among the brokers, the competition is keen for fresh, high quality products. But the best and the freshest are not likely to be shipped to a man known among fishermen as someone less than honest.

The selection from among the twenty-or-so major brokers at Fulton is the fisherman's only marketing decision, unless he owns his own retail shop (as some do), peddles from the back of his truck, or goes door to door. Without those options, he is limited to which broker's tag he pulls from the desk in the packing house and tacks onto the box of iced fish the truck will pick up within a few hours. Ellsworth Sprague, Blue Ribbon, Jos. H. Carter, Inc., M. P. Levy, Caleb Haley & Co., Eastern Seafood Co., Newport

Lobster and Fish Co., Lockwood & Winant, Keeney & Lynch, Montauk Seafood Co. . . . they all have their tags, distributed by every broker to the smallest of shipping points.

Each broker is different, but all are essentially the same. They promise to fight for the highest price to the fisherman (while at the same time they try to convince buyers of the best deal), they promise "same day" returns, meaning the fisherman will have his check within a day or two after the fish are sold, and they promise absolute honesty in counting, weighing and grading whatever product is shipped, from giant tuna to whitebait to littleneck clams to squid to dogfish and octopus. And, with remarkable uniformity, they keep their promises. Over the years, it would make no recognizable difference in a fisherman's income were he to send every box of fish to a different broker each day.

But you will never persuade a fisherman that such is the case. They develop their own broker loyalties (for any number of reasons, including the reception they get when they turn up at a broker's stall at three in the morning — Fulton's busiest hour) and those loyalties persist. Invisible links are established that reach across hundreds of miles, that span the voids of separation and connect Fulton and fisherman with sinews of mutual humanity.

The fisherman makes his set, catches his fish, washes, weighs, ices and boxes them, reaches for a Fulton broker's tag, a hammer and some tacks. Bang, on goes the tag — "We're shipping to Blue Ribbon, boys" — the truck arrives. Four hours later, just after midnight, it pulls into South Street. Ten boxes of striped bass are carted to Blue Ribbon. At 2:30 A.M. they are sold for seventy-five cents a pound to a supplier who stocks the 21 Club and the Harvard Club.

The weather, the date, the proximity of a Jewish holiday, school vacations, the color of the stripers' eyes, a mishap in New Jersey which cost a trap fisherman his haul, and the joke the broker told the caterer, all weave their threads into the indecipherable tapestry of price setting. It happens while the fisherman sleeps, resting from his working day, readying for the next. He'll get his check in the mail the following afternoon — a check he takes, no matter how small. It is Fulton that decides the fisherman's financial destiny — the same Fulton Market that has always made such judgments with such inexplicable formulas.

There are no contracts, no communications, no hard sells, no influence peddling, no advertising, no public relations campaigns, no office managers, no performance charts, no pins in maps, no promises of promotions, no secretaries, no Christmas parties, no stock options, and no keys to the executive washrooms.

But there are sea creatures, rushed to Fulton Market where the emphasis has been on freshness ever since the early days when great wooden boxes floated like so many coffins in the East River off South Street. These were not containers for the dead, but boxes drilled with holes so the river water could circulate and keep the fish in them alive and fresh.

Dealing with a price structure so complex and so abstract that none of Fulton's brokers can fully explain it is the fee the fisherman pays for his freedom. He doesn't ever have to slap a back or shake a cold hand. He catches fish, that's all. Fulton does the rest, as it has been doing for the commercial fisherman since the seventeenth century.

But, during the past fifteen years, there has been a change at Fulton Market, a change more basic than any in its history. The commercial fisherman has become a minority shipper. "Sportsfishermen" have landed fourteen times as much bluefish and bass, thirty-five times as much cod, and that's one more reason why those "same day" Fulton returns haven't always been as good as fishermen have hoped they would be.

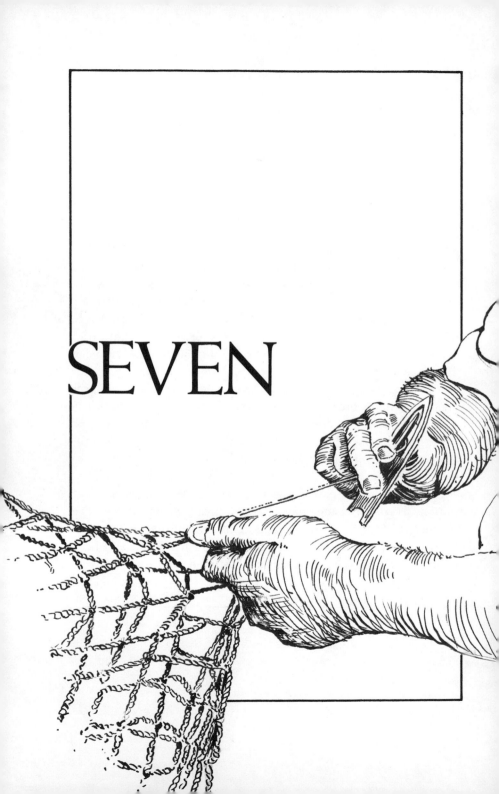

SEVEN

Like the gulls, we follow the fish as they head east along the beach during May and on into the long days of June — that most luminous month. We are up before the sun at three-thirty, ready to set on first light at four, and before another hour has gone, we discuss whether to make a second set. It is not yet five in the morning, but the sun is already bulging orange above the southeast horizon, squat and heavy with its throbbing warmth. Crimson dervishes dart over the slick sea's surface as the sun's velvet reflection stretches, breaks, and moves with the ocean's easy summer undulations.

Sharks follow the warming; we can expect them in the seine in most dawn sets — threshers slapping their scythe tails at the cork line, sand sharks snapping with their ugly, grinning mouths, makos leaping the twine, or crashing through it, and, every so often, hammerheads and blue sharks cruising from wing to wing, their fins slicing the slick surface, slowly at first and then faster as the net tightens and the sharks turn to shred their filmy trap with convulsive bites and the spasmodic turning, twisting and thrashing of their tails. Inevitably, the larger sharks leave us with much mending. We stand there, sweating in our waders as the sun climbs higher, pulsing faster with the fierceness of its heat, and move the needles back and forth, over and under, closing as best we can the open meshes riven by shark teeth. Some mornings I can look down the beach and see the first of the vacationing city bathers running through the surf, splashing and playful. How many, I wonder, would be as abandoned if they had watched the fins moving back and forth within our seine's small arc?

If we escape severe shark damage to the twine, we can make two sets by seven. After that, it is almost too warm to work, and, Ted tells us, the bass move offshore to deeper, darker, cooler waters. We go back, take care of the catch, wait until two or three in the afternoon and return to the beach — a place that is no longer ours. Wherever we go, we are followed by bathers, beach-goers, men, women and children on holiday. They gather and watch, and most of them coo with sympathy for the fish that come writhing in the bunt. We stay silent, removed, dutiful, and as we go about the work, our eyes on the gear and the sand, I look for myself among the watchers, skinny in my bathing trunks, horsing around with Chick and my companions, taking the summer for a playroom, wondering what these men in the rubber suits are doing with June, working, sweating, covered with sand, stinking with fish when they should be in swimming, riding the waves, body-surfing like the me I watch for.

By dusk, the audience thins and vanishes with the sunset. We wait through the long twilight, watching for the flickering of bait fish, a stirring of the waters that may mark the turning of a bull bass moving inshore for his feeding. There is ample twilight to set as late as eight-thirty, and it is often ten by the time we head back to Ted's to end a day that has spanned more than eighteen hours.

We are deranged, in a way, by the sweetness of the season. The weather seems perpetual, the slick ocean caresses the sand instead of pounding it; even the rain is soft, we can fish through it. The days are extruded like golden wire, stretched longer and longer, thinner and thinner, vibrating with the sun's vitality, hot with the friction of their stretching. We walk the golden wire, sustained by the spinning equilibrium of our own excitement at the prospect of more of the same tomorrow. We are like drunkards in a wine cellar, intoxicated as much by the vista of a long row of casks as we are by drinking all our bellies can hold.

But there is no glut of fish. The same heat and the same long sun that keep us sleepless send the striped bass into the cool refuges off the rocks at Montauk. As June pulls past us, even our dawn sets produce barren bunts, flapping sleeves of twine that twitch only with whiptail rays, a sand shark or a handful of sea robins. Ted says we should not be discouraged; he wants to haul right through July and August, pulling his seine across summer until he finds autumn in the net. But Alex must work longer at tending the gardens of his boss's big house, making the roses opulent for the family's July arrival; Peter wants to go purse seining porgies in the bay on Milt's groaning hulk of a dragger. Our spring season ends at a time so rich in the sensual luxury of summer that the sparse call of the geese which began this episode is a needle-slim memory lost in fields of fat grass rippling in the afternoon breeze.

I go to Montauk to find Jim, still working his gear alone, setting gill nets in the bay now, trying for a catch of bluefish before the market is glutted by the July and August arrival of the Point's vast summer schools. I remember what Jim said about charter boats, I recall his stories of the charter skippers he knows, and I ask if he can steer me to a captain who may need a mate.

"Try Al, on the *Skip Too*, over at the town dock," Jim answers after pondering for one of his long pauses. He is sitting on the sand on the beach that runs west of the breakwater, mending a gill net. His shirt is off and his compact shoulders and muscular back are a dark tan. He must already have spent days on this beach, sunning and mending. He will not give up his stubborn search for a system that will make fishing more of a sure thing for him, even if that search forces him to endure days of solitude and discouraging drudgery.

Such a sense of aloneness hovers about him here, working on this sweep of bay beach, bent over his net, fingering every bar in every mesh, compelled by some push within him toward a kind of perfection few, if any, fishermen would consider practical. Jim will mend, and mend again any weakness in his gear because he wants no equipment failures to cloud his testing of the fish. If his nets fail to catch, it will be for other reasons than their readiness and their ability. I feel a kind of guilt that I am not here working with him, staying at the side of the man who let me stay at his when I was useless and knew nothing about fishing, nothing about wood cutting, nothing about working as hard as I have since I learned a fisherman's work.

"Thanks, Cap," I say. "I'll get right over there." Jim nods, the needle moves. "Cap, I'll let you know what he says. How is it going with you? I mean, are you catching enough to pay for your gas? Is it panning out, you fishing alone?"

The needle stops, Jim looks up, smiles. "Finest kind, John, finest kind. Those blues will show here any day, and I'm ready Cap, I'm ready. I'm going to set around on the outside, off Caswell's. I figure those big blues will strike in there first. I'll be shipping them in while the price is still a quarter, instead of a nickel, like it's going to be two weeks later."

"Well, Jim. . . ." I can't quite say it. "Well, if you need any help, you let me know."

"I'm doing fine, Cap. Just like New York." He waves his arm, pointing with the seine needle in his raised hand. "Get on over there and see Al."

The *Skip Too* is a high-sided, V-bottom slab of a charter boat, narrow, rolly, with an unreliable converted Buick engine yanked from a car that rolled over on the Montauk Highway. Al has to use her because he doesn't have the $15,000 it takes to get a charter captain properly started with a newer boat, a dependable engine. He's just a year or so older than I, busting his ass, trying to support a growing family, trying to put enough aside to get a better boat. "One more winter in Florida," he tells me, "if the stock market holds up, and I'll log enough charters for a down payment on a new boat. Then watch me go. Right now, we got to make do with what we have. I want you to know that before I take you on." He stops, gestures at the beat-up fishing chairs, the clean, but worn decks. "Last mate I had figured he wanted to work on a yacht, I guess. Left me high and dry Sunday for a job with a private boat at the club. I had to give up a charter, too.

"What you get is what you see," he says, turning all the way around as he stands in the cockpit talking to me on the dock. "Take a good look. Then, if you still want to mate for me, be here at four in the morning. I got a party for the early tide."

That's how it begins. From that next morning in late June until two weeks after Labor Day, I put in seven days a week aboard the *Skip Too*. We don't miss a day. Even with this slab of a hull, even with Al reluctant to go offshore after tuna, swordfish, and marlin because he doesn't trust the engine, we get charters every day.

Some mornings we watch as the other boats leave. We get depressed as we become one of the two or three charter boats that remain at the dock when the rest of Montauk's hundred-boat fleet has gone. But by noon, something always turns up. A man and his wife walk the docks, looking for a bargain; half-a-dozen Chinese who have driven down late from Chinatown want to go bottom fishing for sea bass off the Elbow. Or we get striper fishermen who figure the afternoon is just as productive as the morning, so why should they get out of bed in the predawn dark and go roll around off the Point while Al trolls back and forth, back and forth over the rips, or works Shagwong, edging the wire lines and lures closer and closer to the bottom where stripers wait in undersea ravines for the tide to tumble baitfish their way.

We are a seagoing taxi, a fish-catching machine, a plane that flies in circles. Al is the captain-pilot, remote, up on the flying bridge, his dark glasses and his preoccupation with navigation put a barrier between him and the passengers. I'm the passengers' man. I'm their stewardess, telling them the rules, making them coffee, tea and drinks, letting out their lines, untangling the snarls. I hook the fish, jig the rods, gaff and boat the fish, gut and clean the fish, make jokes with the parties, tell them fables about the fishing, show them how to work the head, clean up when they puke.

I watch so that they don't fool with trying to readjust the star drag on Al's only reels. I change lures so they'll know we're doing everything we can to catch them more fish. I stand in the rolling cockpit from dawn to dusk when we have morning and afternoon charters. My index finger on my right hand has a permanent slice cut across the side of the middle knuckle where the leader always ends up when I reach over the transom to grab and hold it while I gaff the fish, or yank them into the boat if they're under ten pounds.

If we aren't catching fish, I tell the charters it's only a matter of time; when we do get into fish, I work fast and I make the parties work fast — the more fish they reel in, the more we'll have to throw onto the dock. And the bigger our pile, the more likely we are to pick up a charter for the next day, or the day after.

The thighs of my cotton twill pants are silver and stinking with scales. When we're into a school of small stripers or bluefish, I swing the fish between my legs, then yank the hook from the fish's jaws, toss the lure and line back overboard, then drop the fish in the live well, turn and strip off the line while the passenger holds the rod. That's all they have to do, sit in the chair with the rod butt in the gimbal, turn the crank when the fish hooks itself. Our gear is twice as heavy as it needs to be, the rods are as stiff as steel beams, the leaders are sixty-pound test for ten-pound fish. Al doesn't even slow down for one fish; if we get two on, he eases up. He'll maneuver a bit when we are hit with a tripleheader; he turns around and begins yelling at me, telling me who to move where so the lines won't get tangled and we won't lose our fish.

Fish. That's what this enterprise is about. These charters, these

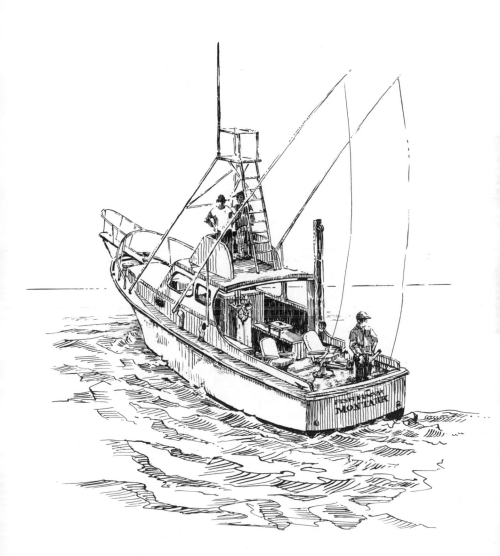

parties, these men and women and children may tell themselves they are off to Montauk for an adventure, for a day on the water, for a look at the lovely blue sky, for a whiff of salt air and some relaxation — a break from the assembly line, a day off from behind the meat counter, a night away from the restaurant kitchen — but they all kid themselves. Once they get aboard, it's fish they are after. If they see fish going silver over the transom of a nearby boat, they turn to me and say, "Hey, they're getting them over there."

They wait in their chairs, their hands trembling on the rods, waiting for that slamming, sudden thump that a big bass makes when it hits. The rod bends, the reel whines and the party goes bananas, yelling, forgetting what he is supposed to do, forgetting what I've told him. Half the time he yanks the hook right out of the striper's mouth; the lure comes aboard with a lip hanging from it.

There are a hundred Montauk charter boats like ours, or better, carrying an average of four to a party. If those four hundred folks don't catch ten fish apiece, it's a bad trip. At two trips a day, which is the average for charters, that's eight thousand bass and blues tossed on the planked docks at Montauk every day. I find myself not believing it, even though I'm gaffing, scaling, gutting and filleting everything the *Skip Too* brings in.

The parties wait in their Dacron shirts and their sandals while a hundred mates like me slice, scrape, behead and disembowel the forty or fifty fish we average on most days. The public docks at Montauk reek with the sweetness of fish guts; the bottom of the harbor is pale with the flayed and rotting carcasses tossed over after the fillets have been slashed away.

I become fish. Their scales are now my skin, their hearts and livers and gonads are squeezed into my clothing. Their muscular writhings at the end of their battles for freedom are permanent tremors in my forearms, thumping as I try to sleep, unable to forget the vitality of the creatures I have pulled up and over the

Skip Too's transom. Fish blood running from the gaff fills my Topsiders; once white, the sneakers turn pale pink, no matter how many times I wash them.

And as I hunch on the dock, my knife cutting through the flesh in my hand, flesh that is mine now as well as that of bass or bluefish, the parties hover, watching to make sure they get theirs, to make certain this mate doesn't slip a fish for himself into some hiding place. And when every fish is cleaned, the parties bring out the plastic sacks they buy at Tuma's and Gosman's and fill them full of wet and slippery fish flesh until, ready to head back to Queens or Brooklyn, they realize they can not lift the bags alone. Three hundred pounds still weighs three hundred pounds.

I watch clumsy struggles to get the trip's catch into the trunks of the cars where the fish will ride, steaming and cooking over the shimmering highways back to the sidewalk front yards. I watch four men from 37th Street put so many bluefish into the trunk of their Pontiac sedan that the back bumper and muffler scrape and squeal on the town dock parking lot as the car goes dragging out, leaving a long white scar in the tar, and a parallel stripe of bloody sea water that sloshes from the trunk as the Pontiac lurches off.

There is a ten-dollar tip in my bloody hand. Al counts his hundred-dollar charter price, gives me another ten dollars and goes to buy some Coke for the next charter, due for the afternoon trip in a half hour.

I turn on the dockside hose as high as the faucet valve allows, haul the nozzle with me aboard the *Skip Too* and try to wash down the decks so cleanly that not a scale or a drop of blood will be left as witness to the morning off Montauk. The boat must be clean for each trip, as if nothing had occurred on the one before. All the charters want to believe they are the first, that this is their particular adventure.

For me, it is always the same.

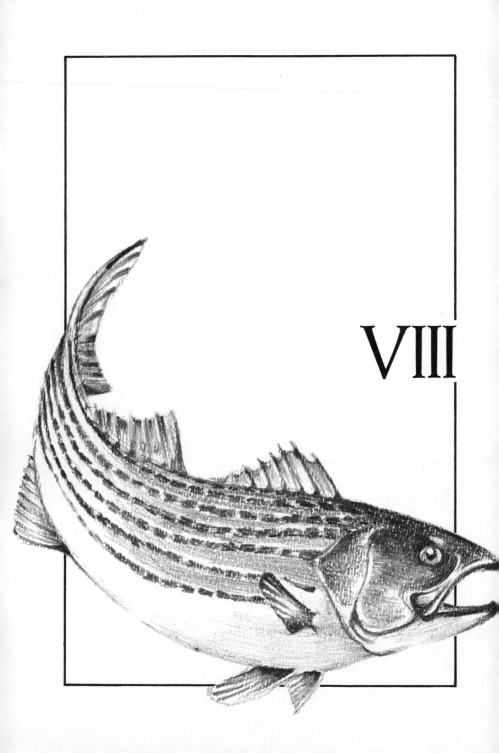

VIII

As American as it is to assign specific dollar values to every presence among us, it is difficult to compute the annual value of the striped bass to the national economy. It is considerable by any standard; that's about all that is known.

One of the problems is measurement. If, for example, one hundred Montauk charter boats land twenty stripers apiece, with each fish averaging ten pounds, the gross cash value of the catch at Fulton Market, where the bass will sell for $1 a pound (the '77 average), computes to $20,000. In the normal two-hundred-day Montauk season, some $4 million worth of striped bass will be boated and shipped.

Montauk is one of dozens of busy charter boat ports that dot the coast from Maryland to Maine — ports that count on the striper as one of their two or three top recreational fish. Twenty ports with catches equal to Montauk's will ship $80 million in stripers to the markets during the May to November season.

Add that total to the take by surfcasters and haul seiners and you begin to establish the base for monetary measurement. But, statistically, you are already in trouble. Any economist will tell you that the value of the catch can not be measured on wholesale prices probably the least significant of the various elements in the charter alone, just as a sociologist will tell you that the price of the fish is fishing mix.

The fleet of a hundred boats at Montauk is worth $1 million according to the local assessors. Most of the skippers who own the boats have homes and real estate in Montauk Village; they buy gas, groceries, equipment and services. Their clients buy lodging, food, liquor and gas to get them down the island. Fishing lures, lines and tackle are expendable and must be replaced at considerable cost. Surfcasters buy all-terrain vehicles, camping gear, flashlights and wet suits. The links in the chain grow farther and farther from the fish they began with. The money builds to billions of dollars.

In 1974, a study commissioned by the National Commission on Water Quality was made by the Department of Economics at Florida State University. Prof. Frederick W. Bell and his colleagues estimated the total market value of the saltwater recreational fishery at something close to $2.5 billion, and climbing, with projections indicating it will hit nearly $4 billion by 1985.

The base for the study is the number of anglers (about 20 million), the number of days they put in as fishermen (about 312 million) and the number of dollars they spend on each of those days for such essentials as bait, beer, boats, and breakfast. The charter boat skipper's contribution to the local economy was not part of the Bell (et al.) computations, nor was the market value of the fish factored in.

Even so, with the striped bass accounting for more than a third of all recreational fishing on the East Coast, some dimensions of its cash value do emerge. Taking the figures that exist, the fish becomes a presence worth hundreds of millions of dollars annually.

The commercial catch (a few million pounds in 1970, compared to nearly 50 million for sportsfishermen in the same year) of bass is seldom added to the mix. Nor is the amount of money commercial men spend for netting, corks, leads, rope, dories, waders, ice, and work gloves. Compared to what recreational fishermen spend for boats, motors, motels, rods, reels, line, lures, booze, docking fees, electronic fish finders, and automatic bilge pumps, the commercial percentage becomes incidental.

In many studies, the West Coast striper is forgotten. But the fish have roamed the Pacific surf ever since that day more than one hundred years ago when the few New Jersey fingerlings that survived their trip by crosscontinent boxcar were released in the tributaries of San Francisco Bay. Fishermen in California and Oregon spend just as much money and time chasing the striped bass as do their eastern counterparts.

But the West Coast casters and trollers have the salmon, which help to ease their longing if the stripers don't show. From Maryland to Montauk, the recreational fisherman counts almost entirely on two inshore species of saltwater fish — the striped bass and the bluefish — and some years the erratic bluefish don't show up. Since the 1930s, the striper has been the pivotal fish for more than half those 20 million anglers tallied by Professor Bell.

But how does one arrive at the value of recreation? How is the benefit of escape measured and quantified? What will happen to a blast furnace tender if he is denied his weekend by the water, the days and nights that allow him to reacquaint himself with Polaris, the curve of a wave, and the sibilance of the surf? These are questions of value which are often asked but seldom answered when recreational fishing is discussed.

The striped bass also has a value as food, which is again not always able to be tabulated in dollars. The *New York Times* food authority, Craig Claiborne, has cooked bass on Gardiners Island for the education of his readers, and proclaimed the fish one of the finest dishes the sea has to offer. The bass shows up on menus at twelve dollars a plate (with almonds) at Le Cirque in Manhattan just one hundred miles from where it was caught by seiners who may have received twenty-five cents for the portion on the restaurant's fine china.

But if food is an elusive category, consider the value of the bass to the scores of writers who have compiled how-to articles for *Field & Stream, Salt Water Sportsman,* and their scores of "out-door" counterparts on the magazine racks and bookshelves. Each year a new flock of readers is told how to find and catch the striped bass; each year the information is essentially the same, only the readers are different. Who has tallied these cash values?

No one has, really, any more than anyone has computed the effects of developing and marketing a new bass lure. But look at Bob Pond of Massachusetts. How different his life (and his income) would have been if he had not created the Captain Bill Bluefish Flash Atom Popper and the boxful of other Atom plugs that are now standard equipment for every bass fisherman. The same is true for the striper addicts who designed the umbrella rig, who deciphered ways surgical tubing can be pulled over a hook, who shepherded the Rebel lures through marketing and corporate battles, who mold plastic worms, or fashion new sorts of knots that can hold the synthetic lines tumbling from DuPont's magical machines.

Ever since Capt. John Smith took note of the striped bass, "thicke" in the shoals of the river mouths he explored, and ever since the bass became a saleable resource of the first Pilgrim settlements, the creature has had a "value" in America. It is a value as abstract and delicate in some aspects as it is computable in others. The bass is the magnet that pulls small groups of men to eastern Long Island beaches at dawn. Drawn there by their mutual love of the sea and affection for the creature, they are caught and pushed together by the net striper spreads — the same lure that attracts the charter-boat fisherman, the surfcaster and the sinker-bouncer snaking a line through a Hudson River sewer grate in an effort at redemption via a meeting with a striped bass.

For three centuries the striper has been the inshore saltwater fish of the northeastern United States. For three centuries the fish has made money for those who have taken it from the sea, or who have outfitted those who do. But if there is a value to these three hundred years, it has not been documented by economists or statisticians. The closest they have come in the American tradition of assigning dollar signs is to tell us the striped bass has an annual value of some several hundred million dollars. That is a considerable amount, but for most fishermen who know the creature, it is not nearly enough.

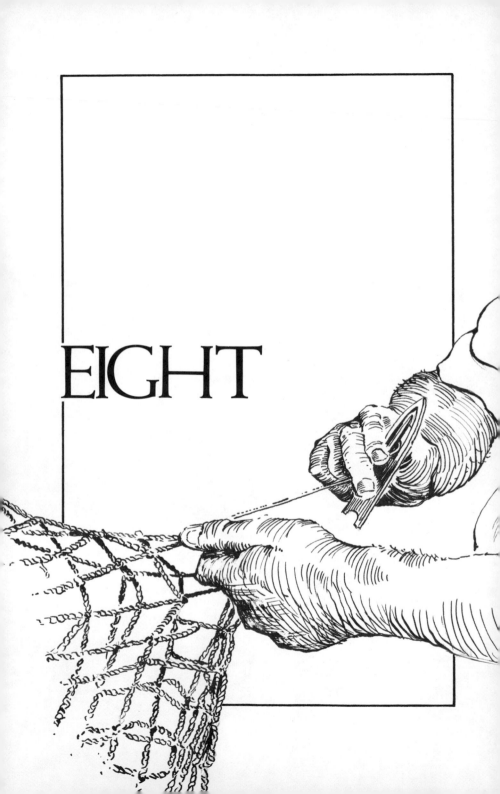

EIGHT

W^e are painting again.

Peter and Jim and I are together for the winter, painting a new house on the west shore of Georgica. It's being built for a concert guitarist from New York. He comes down every now and then to check on progress — an odd but exuberant little man who steps out on the second-story porch on a February day, walks to the rail, opens his fly and begins pissing over the side, turning to explain the process to us as the snow below is sprinkled yellow.

"Good, good. They didn't build the rail too high. This is going to be my bedroom." He turns and sweeps one arm in the direction of the room where Peter and I are working. "I want to wake up in the morning, walk out here on the porch, look out at the ocean, and take my first piss of the day on my own land. That's good, don't you think?"

We laugh and tell Jim the story at lunch. He's not sure he believes it until we take him out and show him the holes in the snow.

We have been here, the three of us, alone, since January. It was not an especially good fall season for any of us. Peter had the best of it. He stayed with Ted. I started with him — the same crew that we had in the spring, Ted, Alex, Peter and I.

But in early November, one evening while we were packing the day's catch — about seven boxes — Jim pulled in with his Rover. He had more than four boxes of bass piled in the back, and he was happy about it.

"I get to keep all mine, Cap," he yelled as he tacked on the shipping tags. "You got to split yours five ways."

I was glad myself, and I know Peter was, to see Jim getting a few fish. It was hard for the two of us, working with Ted, to forget that while we had two trucks and winches, Jim was down east working by himself, rowing, setting, hauling . . . doing it all, full of stubborn determination.

We finished packing about the same time that evening, and Jim stopped me, outside, under the cold stars. He spoke to me softly.

"Cap, those fish are ganging up at the Point now. They're ready to make their move. Could be any day." He put his face closer to mine. In the light of Ted's porch lamp, I could see the intensity in Jim's eyes. "I'm not sure I can handle a good haul by myself. I had trouble with the four boxes I just brought in." He put his hand on my shoulder.

"Remember, John, down at Montauk last summer when you said if I needed any help, I should ask. Well, Cap, I think both of us can do just fine if we get into those bass the day they come around the Point. With my small net, the Rover and the *Peril*, we can fish those beaches to the east that are too small and too rocky for the Poseys and their long seines.

"John, could you drop off Ted's crew? He can get Ding's boy, or Francis, or Brent or somebody to fill in for the rest of the season. He won't have any trouble. Everybody knows the bass are due to strike in any day now.

"I know it too. I'm just afraid that alone I'll lose a bunch. And winter's coming, Cap, winter's coming."

In a way, I wished Jim hadn't remembered what I said. I

mean, it was the kind of thing folks say all the time. "If you need any help, just let me know." But now, I wasn't so sure. First of all, I liked Ted and Peter, and I knew Ted would be hurt and angry at my leaving. He saw Jimmy as competition more than he saw him as a friend. But I thought about what Jim had done for me, about how much had happened since we went to the Main Beach to see Swede on that October afternoon long ago. Jim had never asked me for anything before; I had taken much from him. I said the only thing I figured could be said, even though I had my doubts about Jim's design for fishing.

"Sure, Jim. I mean, I'll give it a try. I will if Ted can get somebody to take my place. We got just a four-man crew you know. I'll go inside and see how he feels about it."

When I walked up the cement steps, holding on to the steel-pipe railing, I was hoping Ted would have some good reason why I should stay with him. But he didn't. He took the move right in stride; he must have had a good many crewmen come and go, as long as he'd been seining.

"So Jim wants you, does he Jawnny? Well, don't blame him. Ain't nobody can handle a rig alone, not if there's any fish along. Besides, Jim and you started together, didn't you? Got to stick by your friends when they need help, ain't that right, Jawnny?"

Ted laughed, tapped me on the shoulder with the back of his sea-swollen hand. "I'll get Brent's boy to come along tomorrow. He's been hanging around here, looking for something to do. Not too much of the season left anyway, is there, Jawn? It ain't enough to worry about."

The next morning was cold. It felt almost as if Jim and I should be heading off to cut wood instead of driving to Gin Beach down near the Point. But Jim was happy with the weather. The bright stars and the frost on the Rover's windshield told him there hadn't been much wind. We could expect a flat sea when the sun started to show in the east, and the cold snap could be the one that would get the bass moving.

Jim was like an architect showing off his new building when

we made the set. I must say, his solo setting had made him ingenious. He demonstrated how the new rollers he had built allowed him to get the loaded dory off the trailer single-handed, and he chattered like a farm wife as we got ready to launch.

"Now, Cap, we tie this line here, like this . . . then over here with this one, through the snap hook, and from there to the Rover winch, ready to haul when we come ashore. Just like New York, Jawn, just like New York."

It was like our beginnings, that set with Jim at Gin Beach, except that both of us had learned more than we had thought there was to know when we first began fishing. We were no longer awkward or unsure; the seine went over easily as I rowed; Jim had no problem with the bunt. But he himself hadn't changed. He was still deliberate, pausing often, making sure, double-checking. The *Peril* rowed easily, as she always had, and while Jim checked the bunt, I had time to look at the eastern sky where the rising sun brought us the first light of a brilliant day. Gulls wheeled over us, and offshore a line of scoters flickered low over the horizon like a last thread of night being blown away. Jim's soft talking to himself was the only sound besides the hushing of the surf as small, regular seas washed at the shore.

I can remember thinking at that moment that I would choose to be no other place, no matter what the options. Making a dawn set in good, autumn weather is fishing at its finest, and fishing is what I like to do best.

After we came ashore we had quite a time, not with the dory, which Jim had learned to handle easily, or with hauling the net. The way Jim had worked out for winching first one wing, and then the other, made hauling relatively easy. We had our time with the fish. A bunch of big bass was in the seine, and we had to strain to get the bunt hauled up high enough to open the cod end.

We had to load the dory with the fish; the back of the Rover wouldn't hold them all. Jim figured we had almost ten boxes, and he was excited and happy. He kept telling me I'd picked the right morning, yelling it as we threw the big slammers into the *Peril*.

"You're some lucky, Cap. That's all I got to say. You're some lucky, Jawn. Down here on your first set with Jim, and we strike into a bunch."

When we got the fish loaded and the net in its proper place, we had to leave the beach for Ted's packing house. There was no way we could make another set with that load of bass in the *Peril*. It took us another two hours to wash, weigh and box the nine boxes we had. We were about to leave to go back east for another try when we heard Peter yelling. He was on top of Ted's big silver truck, helping to guide Ted so he could back in properly. Peter was standing on top of a pile of fish.

"Oh, man, we got them today. We got them, Jim, I tell you." Peter waved his arms, put back his head and laughed. "Oh, John, you wouldn't believe it. This is less than half of what we got. The rest are stacked there on the beach. Must be close to a hundred boxes." Peter threw his cap in the air. "Maybe more. Maybe more."

It was a hard moment. If I had stayed with Ted, I would have been in on the biggest haul of the season. But I had been with Jim; he had asked me to help. Each of us knew what the other was thinking, but neither knew what to say.

Ted got out of the truck. He didn't hesitate: "Get back to the beach, boys. Get back to the beach. There's plenty more bass going by. They're moving today. They're all along the beach, in this pretty weather, too."

Jim and I went back, but by the time we had set again, the fish had moved off. We made two more sets that day, but both of them together didn't add up to a full box. When we got back to Ted's, his crew was still packing. And Peter was still yelling.

"One hundred and six boxes, Cap. One hundred and six boxes, that's what we got here. Oh my Gawd, Johnny, ain't they beautiful."

Peter's natural exuberance, that internal effervescence, was as uncontrollable as a geyser. If he thought about the situation, about what I had just missed, he never said a word. But I don't think he thought about it. For him the joy of such dramatic success was an overwhelming cause for celebration, and celebrating was what Peter liked to do best.

Jim and I left, determined to get up even earlier the next morning. But during the night, the wind breezed up from the southeast; I could hear it rattling the windows as I lay there, awake, thinking about the day just past. When I heard the windows, I knew there would be no fishing in the morning. There wouldn't be weather.

That sou'easter was the start of a ten-day blow. It was December before any of us could get back on the beach, and by then the main body of fish had gone by. None of the crews did much. Jim and I quit the afternoon we hauled in just two blind bass; Ted and Peter and the rest put their nets away two days later.

Soon after Christmas, we three got this painting job.

I like it for several reasons, but mostly for its location. Standing on the upper porch (where the owner tested the rail's dimensions) I can look south, down the length of Georgica to the Gut, and beyond the Gut is the ocean, rolling in, always. To the east, on clear days, I can make out the white chimneys of the house on the dunes. Sometimes I feel as if I am standing out in front of myself, looking at all of my life, the way I sometimes look into shop windows.

On an early March afternoon, shortly after the day we quit early for my thirty-second birthday, I think I hear geese calling from beyond the dunes. I run to tell Peter, who joins me, listening, on the porch. But we never see the birds.

"I think you're making this up, John," Peter says, looking up, turning, to scan the golden sky. "No geese yet. Too early. Too damn cold. But you can't wait, can you, John? You want to get back to that beach. Doesn't make any difference if you get sand in the crack of your ass, or damn near drown trying to catch a few fish. You'll sleep about two hours a night, work about twenty hours a day, just to get out there and get soaked in the surf. Now ain't that right, Johnny, ain't that right? You'll do anything to keep fishing, won't you? Even if you don't make any money."

"I would. You're right, Peter. I would do just about anything. But I'm not sure I'll be able to go this spring. I don't know. . . ."

Peter interrupts. "What! You're not sure? Come on, Cap. What are you saying?"

"What I'm saying is, I may not be able to stay here. My father, you know, he's got the same name. I'm a junior. Well, he's been getting a slew of my bills. He says the store people keep after him because they know he's got the money.

"Well, I do have a bunch of bills. There's no question about that. You know we haven't made any money to speak of, not since we started. I mean, no real money. Not enough extra for paying bills."

Peter still can't believe it. "But John, what are you going to do? Where else can you go and make more?"

"I haven't said much about it, Peter, but my father has been pressuring me to get a job, to 'use my college training,' as he puts it. He called me a couple of days ago and said he has a friend who runs a company. They may have a job for me."

"But what kind of a job, John? And when would it start? Christ, I didn't know about any of this."

"I know, I know. I didn't want to talk about it. I kept hoping it wouldn't happen. You know what I mean. But, shit. The old man has a point. We've been fishing for years now, and we still can't make any money. I didn't give a damn about going into debt. Fishing is so much fun. It's all I can think about. But I can't make believe any longer. I mean, we're just not making it work, Peter. God damn it, I wish I could understand how the Poseys do it. They make a living."

Peter puts down his brush, looks out over the rail, toward the Gut. "They do it different, John. It's all they know, and they know it better than anyone else ever will. It's in their blood, they have a sixth sense, about the weather, about the water, about what fish are moving. You and I could live on the beach for a hundred years and we still wouldn't know what the Poseys know. The thing is, they don't even know they know it. It's part of them, like their arms and legs. They think everybody has the same understanding. They think everybody is born knowing how to mend net, or build a skiff, or tong for clams. And they can't understand when you and I can't do it. They don't even know we can't, really. The Poseys look right at us and see two men in waders, so they figure we know what there is to know about fishing, or we wouldn't be doing it.

"Well, we don't know. And, in some ways, we'll never learn. There's too much mystery there, too much that has to be born in you. But I sure as hell have had a good time fishing, haven't you? And I've learned some things the Poseys never thought I would. I've learned about work, about the water, and about men like you and Jim. I still can't mend net worth a shit, but I'm glad we did what we did."

Jim walks out on the porch, looks around, bemused that we're not painting. "What is this? I didn't hear anyone say coffee time. Besides, I'm the one that says coffee time around here." Then Jim walks off the porch, comes back, and in a stage whisper, says, "Coffee time."

It's a routine we've been sharing for years. It still gets a smile. Peter tries to explain.

"You may know more than I do, Jim, but I just heard from John that he may not be going fishing this spring. His father is putting the pressure on him to get out of debt, wants him to get a job."

Jim has known about the debt. To him, it has always been a sign of sloppiness on my part. He says as much. "You made your bed, Cap. You're the one that has to lie in it."

"But Jim," Peter says, "what are you going to do without your partner? Who will crew for you if John goes?"

"I'll get along, I'll get along." Jim looks over our heads, at some plan he's been designing while he's been swinging a paint brush for the past two months. "I may not even go on the beach. I've been thinking I might cut that seine back into gill nets, put a well and an outboard in the *Peril* and set the nets over in back of Tobacco Lots, in the bay. They tell me the bass and blues come in there every spring, and there's nobody around to bother them."

Peter knows the place. "Hey, Cap, that's not a bad idea. Milt and I been out that way, chasing scup. Looks fishy to me. You'll get 'em, Cap, you'll get 'em."

We start back inside, but Peter stops just at the door. He flashes that wide, white-teeth smile, that irrepressible zest of his. "I wasn't going to say anything until later, until we finished this job. But now that John says he's going to have to go, I better let you know. I'm going to California, where my mother's family is, near San Francisco. They say there's a load of money to be made. People are moving in by the thousands. They want to build houses on the family land. I'm going to be a real estate tycoon, that's what I'm going to be. As soon as we get done here, I'm going."

Dusk is coming on. It's time to go out back by the paint shed, time to wash the brushes in kerosene, shake them out and wrap them carefully in cheesecloth, the way Jim has taught us.

I look down toward the Gut, toward the white chimneys. I see myself and Peter rowing in the dark of the night set with Ted. I see myself and Jim and Swede lifting my first ever gill net; I feel the first bass in my hand. I see myself and my brother Chick racing over the dunes, enjoying the boyhood adventures that I have tried to extend. I see the baby in those brown hands, being lifted from the surf, blinking, hearing the laughter of the servant girls.

We bang our brushes on the side of the shed, shaking out the drops of kerosene. The sun is down, the sky is dark in the east, still pink in the west. We wrap the brushes carefully. Peter starts for his pickup; Jim and I head for the Rover. I call out to Peter.

"So long, Cap. See you in the morning."

"You bet, Jawn, you bet."

Peter starts up the truck, pulls out onto the road. Jim turns on the Rover ignition key, waits while the fuel pump works, then turns to me, looks hard at me. "So you two are really leaving," he says.

"Yes, Cap. It looks that way, don't it."

Jim starts the Rover, and we head for home, past the dunes, past the Main Beach, past the big houses with their clipped privet hedges and long, bluestone drives.

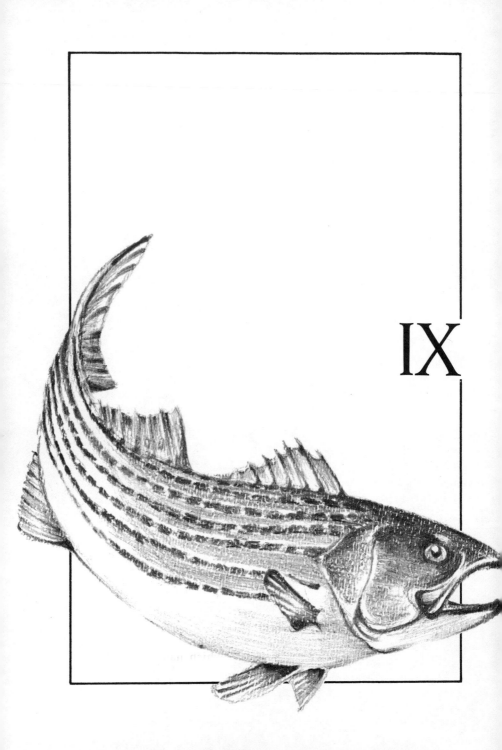

IX

Ever since John Smith made his journal notes about the vast presence of striped bass in the rivers and estuaries of the New World, Americans have recorded in some fashion the comings and goings of the coastal creatures. Few have done it in a scientific manner, however, and as a result it has been difficult to trace fluctuations in the striper population during the past three hundred years. "Records" from the early days consist either of enthusiastic, albeit unspecific, observations like Smith's, or of the accurate, but narrow, registers of some of the striped bass fishing clubs which duly note every bass taken by every club member and guest, but seldom mention how other clubs and commercial fisheries compare.

Such casual accountings have made it all but impossible for contemporary scientists to make irrefutable trend analyses of bass populations. There are, nevertheless, several basic conclusions about striper populations on which the body of observers does agree. One of them is that there has been a general decline in the number of fish on the East Coast since 1885. From the 1600s until just before the start of the twentieth century (so goes the scientific consensus), stripers generally held to the numbers which had prompted such wonder in Capt. Smith. In the 1920s there was some recovery, but it was not until 1936 and '37 — when the 1933 and '34 year classes reached maturity — that stripers made enough of a population comeback to reassert their general popularity and availability.

But even those fat years, it should be noted, bulged with bass in numbers that had been taken for granted a century before. According to Edward C. Raney, chief author of the definitive scientific text on the stripers, bass populations tend to run in periodic cycles. Every six years or so, there is a hatch and survival rate which sends the population soaring. Ironically, this little-understood phenomenon appears to occur when bass numbers are at their lowest — in other words, just when they need a large, new, year class. The numbers show, however, that even when fish get lucky and a significant portion of the eggs survive and hatch, the balance will not achieve the numbers of the population boom that most recently preceded it.

While the striper population goes up and down fairly regularly, each "up" is a notch or two lower than the one before it. According to Maryland Department of Natural Resources fisheries biologist, Joseph G. Boone — who has kept scientific population records of year-class fry born in the Chesapeake tributaries — excellent reproduction occurred in the forties, early fifties, and in 1956, '58, '64, '66, and, finally, in 1970.

Since the start of this decade, the news from the Chesapeake — the nursery which incubates 90 percent of the East Coast's stripers — has not been good. It has, instead, been the story of a striper-spawning disaster, a disaster which is reflected in the growing number of articles appearing in the fishing and popular press, as well as in professional fishery bulletins.

If the six-year pattern for a bass population boom is considered reasonably regular (as it is by contemporary marine biologists) then the stripers are currently two years overdue for a spawning explosion.

More and more striper watchers are waiting for the boom which has not yet come, but the latest news from the Chesapeake is glum indeed. Not only have billions of larval bass failed to survive, but they have died in such huge numbers that there are scarcely any new bass joining the schools of their brethren. After a search for survivors of the spring-of-1977 breeding frenzy in the Nanticoke and Choptank, Joe Boone reported fewer bass fry in his research seine than he had ever counted before, and he has been making the surveys since 1958.

The news from Maryland, plus the dwindling catches put on docks and in packing houses from North Carolina to Maine, has begun to alarm both commercial men and sportsfishers. Johnny Kronuch, who has sold surfcasting equipment from his Montauk shop for more than two decades, said at the end of the 1977 season, "We got skunked. . . . We're completely dead. I'm running out of ideas why." Haul seiners from Amagansett and the Hamptons made their money from bluefish and weakfish during the same season; a catch of more than two hundred pounds of bass was a rare haul; twenty years ago, two thousand pounds of bass in a set would hardly be considered a catch worth mentioning.

Stories and headlines began to appear on the sports pages of several coastal New England papers. Of these, the headline which appeared in the *Providence Sunday Journal* (Nov. 6, 1977) is typical. It reads: "The striped bass, king of gamefish, may be vanishing from the coast." Surely a catalyst for the report was the failure of the annual Rhode Island Striper Tournament to produce a single bass, even though hundreds of surfcasters and boat fishermen tried for several days to land one. In past years, the same event has produced thousands of pounds of the fish.

What bass are being taken are large — the last survivors of the huge year classes of the fifties and sixties. These twenty-five- to sixty-pound fish are wise, relatively scattered, and are not likely to be located or taken in any concentrations. From the fat years just after World War II, when the technologists produced all manner of devices for luring and catching the striper, the fishery has become a shadow of its former numbers. Once a reliable and productive source of food and recreation for the millions, the striper has indeed all but vanished from the coast.

Bob Pond of Attleboro, Massachusetts, who makes, or did make, a good share of his living from the manufacture and sale of striper lures, is also president of Stripers Unlimited, a national organization devoted to the preservation and multiplication of the species. Last summer, Bob Pond petitioned the U. S. Department of Commerce to add the striped bass to its endangered species list — a move intended to spark more governmental interest in researching the alarming and sad decline of striper populations.

Pond was turned down because the Department is still waiting to see if one more spring in the Chesapeake won't produce a bonanza year class. John Smith would be incredulous at what has become of the fish that were once so thick he could walk dry-shod on their backs across a river mouth.

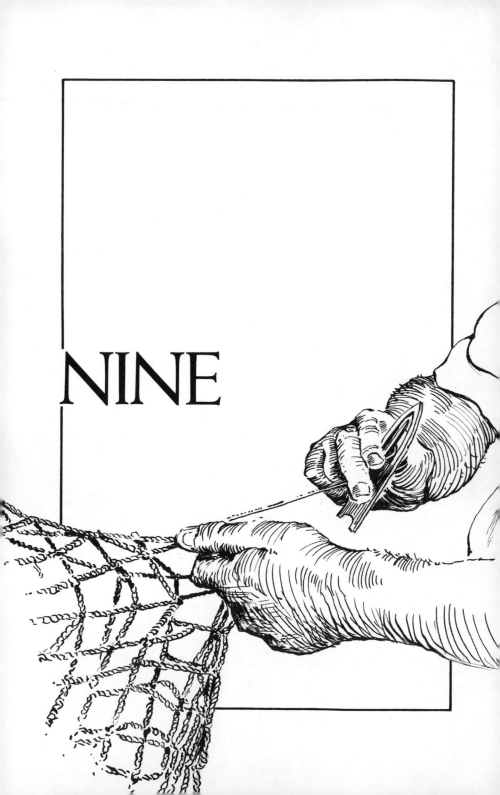

NINE

I am in Maine. We did leave, the two of us, Peter and I. For us, the fishing was over.

But not for Jim. He stayed. He stayed and tried, and kept trying. Once every three or four years, I would go back; I always stayed with Jim. He had the Rover and the *Peril* in his yard, twine hung from lines; his house was surrounded by anchors, flag buoys, corks, all manner of fishing material, stacked neatly, precisely, each piece in its proper place. I would wake in the dark of the dawn and hear Jim moving in his kitchen, making coffee, grabbing a doughnut from the box he had bought the evening before. Sometimes I would go with him, to give him a hand lifting his gill nets, or to work with him at whatever new fishing system he was trying at the time. He never gave up; he was still alone.

I didn't hear from Peter much after he went to California. There were one or two phone calls, right away, within weeks of his arrival, when I would get drunk at night and call to hear Peter laugh, to have him tell me stories about the weather there, the houses that were going up, the money he was making.

I was watching the late news on television, lying on my bed in the old Maine house I lived in then, when I next heard from

California. Peter had been there about three years. The phone rang; I turned down the TV volume and picked up the receiver.

This thin, wavering voice — a voice I did not know — began trying to tell me that Peter was dead, that he had died in an automobile accident, gone off a mountain, or something, the voice said, on his way back from a day skiing.

I said no, it could not be Peter. Peter was too full of life, too exuberant, too charged with the tumult of his personal joy to die in a violent accident, to drive off a mountain. I could not comprehend the news. But I said thank you for letting me know to the caller, yes, I had fished with Peter, yes, he was a friend, yes, I was the right John that he talked about.

I hung up the phone, and went to turn the television volume up, but I could not. I lay there on my bed the rest of the night while the set hummed, and I thought about Peter. I kept trying to put him back together in my head. I wanted so to see him as he had been. Jesus Christ, his spirit was so huge. When I was with him, his joy of living spread over me like a magic cape. Together we could fly.

Truly, he had died. The next day, I called back because I still could not comprehend. I talked with his mother, who had been a girl in that house west of ours on the dunes, that airy house where my spirits had been set so free. She told me Peter had not been happy in California, that he kept saying he was, that he kept his laughter loud, but that his days had been full of a busy aimlessness, that he had started drinking more, skiing faster, driving faster. Then she told me she believed in her heart that Peter had driven himself off the mountain. He wanted to live no longer.

I rocked through the following days and nights, grieving, grieving for Peter's desperation, for his loss of joy, grieving for the end of fishing and the separation that had come to this.

I did not hear from Jim during that time. I did not see him again for about three years. Then I went back to the East End and Jim took me fishing off the Point in his gillnetting boat — a lovely boat some Chesapeake Bay fisherman had built for him. We fished through a northeaster; the wind blew up enough to keep most of the charter boats at the dock. But Jim said that was good.

"Those big bass, those slammers, they love the wind nor'east. Stirs them right up, Cap. Put that line over. We'll take a turn around Number Five, scrape one of those slammers off the bottom."

Jim made the turn around the buoy, and we had a fish on, a good one. After half an hour it came alongside, hung there, rising in the swells, almost at eye level — a thirty-pound striper, suspended there like a topaz in the emerald sea. Jim had no gaff; he had not been rod-and-reel fishing for years, and the fish was too large to hoist aboard by a leader that was certain to break. I leaned way over the gunwale in the choppy seas, trying to work my hand into the fish's gills. I touched the cold, striped side of the bass. He whipped his wide tail convulsively, then broke off the hook. For a moment, the fish did not realize it was free; he and I were each caught in the intensity of the event. A swell lifted Jim's boat, the bass rippled like a wave, moved away, and was gone.

"Can you believe that, Cap? No gaff. Imagine, me not having a gaff aboard." Jim looked at me with those intent blue eyes for a long moment, then he smiled. "Now what prompted that? Me, Jim, out here without a gaff."

I didn't mind. I really didn't. We had the fish caught. I was relieved to see it break off, to go on living. It was growing too rough to fish much longer. We were the only boat under the light. We headed in, sliding down the long, following seas from the northeast. Jim kept talking about the missing gaff all the way to the breakwater.

That was in the fall, October. In February, on my birthday, while I was sitting at my birthday dinner table with my wife and children, the phone rang. It was a call from the East End.

Jim had been trying to move some of his fishing gear out of the snow, had been pushing hard, had been hit with a heart attack, taken to the hospital where he had died. The voice on the phone said, "Just like his father on the train. No warning. Boom. Jim had been told it could happen."

I hung up the phone, put my head down on the dinner table and sobbed. I couldn't help it. The children sat there, awkwardly, hurting for me, embarrassed by me, not knowing what else to do but sit and wait for me to stop.

I did stop, after a while. I wondered what had brought the tears so fast. I hadn't been seeing Jim all that much. I had never broken through to the part of him he kept so private. But he, of all the people I knew in the world, had been my friend. When I met him that October afternoon at the Main Beach and we began fishing with Swede, Jim made room for me in his life, took me through the fishing adventure, was at my side while I grew up, and would have stayed at my side for as long as I needed him.

I cried too for his stubbornness — the stubbornness, in a way, that had killed him at fifty-one. Oh, Jim. How he wanted to beat fishing, how he wanted to succeed as a fisherman. He could have been a fine musician, a good furniture designer, an exceptional carpenter and painter, but he only wanted to be a fisherman. He tried, God dammit, he tried every day for twenty years; he tried until his heart burst.

Jim's wife asked me to speak at his memorial service, so I drove alone to New London and took the ferry over, watching the gulls, looking for a sign of fish, even though I knew it was early yet.

I talked about how hard Jim had tried, and about how much he cared about the East End and what its ocean and beach and wild places had given both of us, who had come there as young men from a city just a hundred and twenty miles away to find ourselves, together, in a dory.

After the talk, Francis, one of the Poseys, came up to say hello. He couldn't talk much because he missed Jim too. But I asked him about Ted and he told me Ted was doing poorly, not fishing anymore.

I drove to Ted's yard. It seemed strange, arriving there in the brilliance of noon. The same shells were crushed in the drive, the big silver truck was parked there; and the dory and seine were nearby. I walked up the cement steps in my city shoes and into the kitchen where so many dawns had come to us, there in our waders, drinking instant coffee and eating toast spread with Ted's peanut butter.

Ted was in the living room, lying on the sofa. "I ain't too good, Johnny," he said to me when I asked. It was difficult talking to him when he was down. I had never seen him down before. He was always up, full of fire, like Smiley once said, wanting to catch every fish in the ocean.

"Do you get to the beach much?" I asked, trying to make some kind of small talk.

"No, Johnny. The boys are running the rig now. I let them have it. They do a good job of it, too. Been catching a few. Nothing like we did though, Johnny. Nothing like we did." He turned his head to look right at me.

"Johnny, I still wake up every morning. Can't sleep past four o'clock, even with them pills. I hear the truck start up. . . . Oh, Gawd, Johnny, I want so to be there."

I watched Ted's blue eyes fill with tears. The eyes I had always thought so hard were awash with his sadness. I couldn't stay. I couldn't take it.

I went out, down the steps and into the seine shed. I didn't want anyone to see me. Christ, what's happening here? First Peter, then Jim, and now Ted. I survive, I'm the only one. My friends, my crew, my companions, the men I have come to love the most . . . they're gone. I've got a whole, long stretch left to go now without them. What the fuck, what do I do now? My life is all departures, no arrivals.

I came back to Maine, alone. In two months, I read in the *East Hampton Star* that Ted had died of cancer.

I go out alone in my small dory, on the bay here, when the

season is right, and I fish for stripers. I have a light casting rod. I work small surface plugs, mostly. I love to see the fish rise and swirl. Sometimes I just drift, when I find a bunch. I let the boat glide slowly over them. If the tide is right, and there is not too much wind, I can lean out over the bow and look down, right into a school of stripers.

There they are, in these clear Maine waters, flashing, turning, their silver bellies showing. Light and dark flash in that submerged world I can never quite reach. I drift with the school for as long as I can, riding their beauty and their vitality back to the East End, back to the mornings, back to the Gut, back to the white chimneys, back to Ted's big sea hands, Jim's long blue-eyed look, Peter's joyous shout, back to seeing myself rowing a big, haul-seining dory through the open surf of the Atlantic.

The wind shifts, my drift ends as the bass wheel, shine, flash again, and are gone.

I row home, to my Maine home, to the chores, to the different life I live here now. I think to myself how good it is that the striped bass have followed me here. In them, I can find something of what I discovered and all that I have lost.

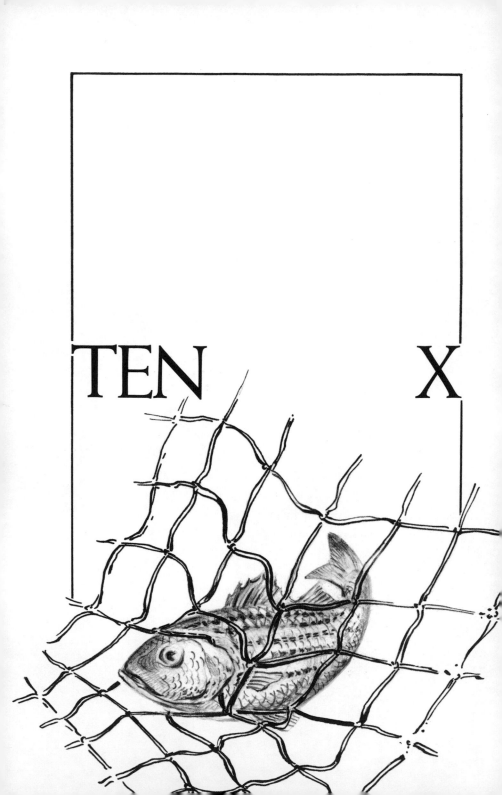

TEN   X

So there is death here too, as fish and man come together.

Yet it is the striped bass that has given me life. Through seven years at the rim of the Atlantic with this fish as the primary focus of my work, I have pulled together the values that have held my being in place ever since. I have not only survived, I have lived.

I want to pay my dues. I want some attention given to the striper. I want decisions made to halt the extinction of *Morone saxatilis*. Because, after uncounted centuries as a presence on the east coast of this nation, the striped bass is dying. This fish, once so abundant it clogged river deltas, this resource of such economic importance that its sale helped fund the first public school in America, this creature whose poetry has nourished the souls of men since the Indians, this natural presence of a natural god is being destroyed.

In the process are the patterns of man's own destruction. Just as the striper saved me, if we work to save the fish, we may ourselves be saved.

We begin by debating the dying.

There is no debate about the decline in striped bass populations since 1970. Annual surveys of bass reproduction in Chesapeake Bay and the Hudson River, made by trained biologists like Joe Boone, tell the same story each spring and fall. These two bodies of water — which together are the nurseries for 99 percent of the stripers on the northeast coast — have been increasingly unproductive each year of this decade. There is no debate about that fact, not among scientists, not among statisticians and not among recreational and commercial fishermen.

The debate is over why these waters should be failing. The arguments are about why even the stubborn striper, with its high tolerance for pollution and its courageous compulsion to reproduce, should have faltered in its purpose. Why, when the Nanticoke and the Choptank are sweet with the smell of the striper's rites of spring; why, when the waters of the Wicomico are cloudy with the billions of eggs cast by leviathan cow stripers; why is there no surviving year class? Why, instead, does the creature's population decline until now the rivers and sea hold only a handful of old fish — fish that gather each April for a sterile ritual of reproduction, an act of consummate irony that ends when the childless parents leave their spawning grounds believing they have fulfilled their obligations when, instead, they have birthed only millions of minute corpses: their suffocating fry.

Faced with the statistics of the alarming death rate, many scientists simply say there is no explanation — not any that is known. Some commercial fishermen, not wanting to believe in the mortality of their mainstay, will tell you that the bass have moved, have sought the dark, central depths of the open ocean where they will tend to their own restoration, and someday return. Still other fishermen — some who are scientists and some who are not — will say there is no cause for alarm. "These are just fluctuations," they say. "The bass will make a comeback."

But for me there is no escape into romance, wishful thinking, mystery, or the "not-to-worry" rationalization of anxiety. I am, along with many others, quite certain now that the striped bass is being destroyed by the effects of the toxic chemicals which have penetrated every creek and tributary of the Chesapeake and every mile of the Hudson accessible to the fish.

Consider the evidence. The Chesapeake is a vast, flat saucer of shoal water. As William Warner tells us in his book *Beautiful Swimmers,* "The Bay's entire watershed extends north through Pennsylvania to the Finger Lakes and Mohawk Valley country of New York, by virtue of the Susquehanna, the mother river that created the Bay in Pleistocene time. To the west it traces far back into the furrowed heartland of Appalachia, but one mountain ridge short of the Ohio-Mississippi drainage, by agency of the Potomac. To the east, the flatland rivers of the Eastern Shore rise from gum and oak thickets almost within hearing distance of the Atlantic barrier islands. To the south, Bay waters seep through wooded swamps to the North Carolina sounds, where palmettos, alligators, and great stands of bald cypress first appear."

The bay proper is the captive of the land that surrounds it, with just one slim outlet to the sea at Cape Charles and a man-made canal to the north. Yet some of the most intensive farming and industrial production in the nation occupies the land around the Chesapeake, and from both activities over the past fifty years, rivers of chemicals have run in floods into the bay between them. Into no other large, shallow estuary in the world have so many residual chemicals found their way. On the one hand, the rain washes the agricultural land of the pesticides, herbicides, and fertilizers which Eastern Shore farmers use with increasing abandon as pressures for production mount. On the other hand, the northern edge of the bay is blackened with the manufacturing plants of the DuPonts and their counterparts. From these industrial complexes in the Delaware and Maryland manufacturing heartland, chemical wastes have gushed into the Chesapeake for decades.

And the Hudson is no better. Many will say it is worse. The most recent study of chemical pollutants in the Hudson, a report jointly issued in October 1977, by the Environmental Defense

Fund and the New York Public Interest Research Group, says, "[T]he river is awash with deadly chemicals, and it gets worse every day." But even before that report was issued, New York authorities had banned the sale of most species of Hudson fish (including striped bass) because their flesh contained such high levels of chemicals known to be harmful to humans. One has only to take a census of the industries that operate over the length of the Hudson to comprehend how a river of its scope can be converted to a chemical carryall.

So for me, there is no debate. If the only two bodies of water on the northeast coast where the striped bass is known to breed in significant numbers — if the only two striper nurseries yet discovered which produce the great, migrating populations that have awed people since before the time of Capt. John Smith — if these two places are also the two most chemically tainted major bodies of water in the northeast, then the miracle for me is that the bass still survives. Consider the courage and the persistence of a creature that has suffered such corrosion of its habitat and still tries to coexist with its corruptors.

I have difficulty comprehending such courage, just as I have difficulty understanding the inertia and resistance in private and public agencies over the plight of this creature. Have we indeed reached a point in these waning days of the industrial age when we will allow the demise of an entire species without so much as an expression of concern, an effort to reverse the sentence? If we have, we have signed our own death warrants. There can be no extrication of the fate of fish from the fate of man. We are one and the same. That is a truth I discovered in the wash of the ocean waves.

To me, apathy about the bass is inexplicable, particularly in the face of the evidence of crisis that has been published during recent years. Consider some of the following:

• ITEM: Hundreds of dead and dying bass washed up on shores of Long Island Sound during the last two weeks of September

1977. Subsequent research (undertaken and funded by concerned sportsfishermen) into the causes of the vast kill revealed an abnormal "Andromeda strain" bacterial pathogen which caused a grotesque enlargement of the bass kidneys. The mutant bacteria are thought to be generated by the presence of a toxic chemical.

- ITEM: Virginia's St. James River was closed to fishing in December 1975. Shortly after, the factory which produced the toxic chemical pesticide, Kepone, was also closed. Kepone had been identified as the agent that tainted the fish. Recent surveys show that the chemical is still so prevalent that the river will have to be closed to fishing at least until 1980.
- ITEM: A study in 1977 by marine scientists found that the New York Bight and parts of Long Island Sound are contaminated by extraordinary levels of heavy metals. The findings, which report contamination as much as several thousand times the norm, followed reports by sports and commercial fishermen of nearly barren inshore fishing grounds that contributed to the worst summer of fishing in memory.
- ITEM: During the summer of 1977 the Federal Food and Drug Administration issued orders prohibiting the sale of striped bass with certain levels of PCBs (polychlorinated biphenyls) in their flesh. Fishermen fought the restriction because so many bass had absorbed enough PCBs to make them unsaleable.
- ITEM: According to the *New York Times* (Sept. 8, 1977), "Pollution has turned the once abundant Atlantic fishing grounds off Long Island, New York City, and New Jersey into a foul and nearly barren sea."
- ITEM (from the *Federal Register*): "Three problem areas are of major concern to the Food and Drug Administration, namely the new toxicity data on PCBs, studies that indicate PCBs are carcinogenic, and the presence of PCBs in the environment resulting in widespread occurrences of residues in fish."
- ITEM: "The brain, muscle, unfertilized ova, or testes from

striped bass... collected in 1973 from each of eight study streams along the Atlantic Coast from the Nassau River, Florida, to the Hudson River, New York, were analyzed for nine organochlorine residues: levels of DDT (dichlorodiphenyl trichloroethane), PCBs (polychlorinated biphenyls), dieldrin, cis-chlordane, toxaphene, mirex, HCB (hexachlorobenzene), BHC (benzene hexachloride), and DEHP (di-2-ethylhexyl phthalates). In 1974, organochlorine residue levels were also determined in muscle, unfertilized ova, and 24-hour prolarvae from hatchery brood fish collected from two of the study streams.... Fish of the 1973 collection were also analyzed for metals: mercury, selenium, arsenic, cadmium, and lead.

"All females from the 1973 stock contained PCB Aroclor 1254, dieldrin, and p,p¹ DDT or its degradation products. Striped bass from... the Middle Atlantic drainage area... contained residues of HCB with PCB Aroclor 1242. Fish from one or more rivers within the South Atlantic drainage area were contaminated with cis-chlordane, toxaphene, mirex, and DEHP....

"For most pesticides, the ova of females carried the heaviest residue.... Mercury, selenium, arsenic, cadmium, and lead were geographically widespread contaminants occurring in the brain, muscle, unfertilized ova, or testes of all 1973 stocks of striped bass. Arsenic in the ova of [fish from the] Nanticoke River ranged up to 3.7 μg/g. [From McBay, Hogan and Schoettger, 1977, *Organochlorine and heavy metal residues in striped bass*, U.S. Fish & Wildlife Service report.]"

There is enough material for another entire book of such "items." During the course of my mounting concern for the creature I care for, I collected scores more. The evidence is documented and overwhelming. What bothers me most is the failure of an essentially humanitarian republic to respond to such an apparent threat, not only to the striped bass, but to us all.

The same sorts of chemicals were proved to have caused sterility among a dozen male workers at the Occidental Chemical Company in Lathrop, California. Their task there was to blend an amber-colored liquid called dibromochloropropane (DBCP) that is used, on the farms around the Chesapeake and across the nation, to kill microscopic worms in vegetable fields. Sperm counts in those workers had dropped to zero after just a few years of employment at the factory.

According to a report in the *New York Times* (Sept. 11, 1977), after the sterility tests became public knowledge, "DBCP became the villain in what has developed as one of the most dramatic, clear-cut, and widespread instances of environmental contamination since public attention began focusing on the matter in the 1960s.

In recent days, since people have learned that DBCP is linked not only to sterility, but also to cancer, the problem has assumed nationwide dimensions. It may involve tens of thousands of factory workers and field hands. . . . Because of all this, the affair has raised a flock of serious questions to which, so far, there are no clear answers. The biggest one, perhaps, is this: How many other toxic chemicals have similarly invaded the environment . . . undetected, their dangers unappreciated?

Further reports in the *Times* and other publications had some answers to the questions. DDT and PCB residues were found in the breast milk of nursing mothers — fourteen hundred in forty-six states, after tests by the Environmental Protection Agency. And the La Leche League joined the Environmental Defense Fund in recommending that pregnant mothers eat no freshwater fish, or fish — like the striped bass — that frequent inshore and fresh waters.

More toxic chemicals were found in a herd of Michigan cows, and toward the end of the year, a report was issued from New Orleans saying that a team of Tulane University scientists had de-

termined that PCBs in drinking water can affect (and possibly
have affected) the functions of the human brain. Even the smallest
amounts of the chemical, which the scientists found primarily in
fish, can contribute to learning disabilities in children by altering
hormone levels in the brain.

Enough is enough is enough. Documentations, reports, ex-
amples, analyses could roll here for pages. But I don't believe it is
necessary. I believe there are enough people with enough common
sense to read the evidence at hand, to look the facts full in the face,
and comprehend the simple truth that there is no such thing as a
free lunch. We can not chemically destroy even a microscopic
vegetable worm without destroying a part of ourselves. We can not
utilize the waters of the northeast as chemical sewers without destroying the integrity of those waters.

That we have done, and, in the process, we have destroyed
that particular and graceful swimmer of the surf, the striped bass.

Thus far, even in the face of the steep decline in bass populations and the mounting concern of sport and commercial fishermen,
there has been little if any governmental action, either at the state
or federal level. Instead, in what is, for me, an incredible arro-
gance, public agencies have moved the opposite way. The New
York State Assembly, which had previously established deadlines
which would end offshore dumping off Long Island, reversed its
stand and repealed the measure. The dumping will not only continue, but will grow worse.

The same sort of insensitive ignorance is mirrored in Washington where Elliot Richardson, former Secretary of Defense, and
now U.S. representative to the Law of the Sea Conference at the
United Nations, has clashed with the Carter Administration and
the Environmental Protection Agency over a proposed ban on
dumping anything within two hundred miles of the coast. Richardson wants dumping to continue unhindered either by public concern or by laws.

And the U.S. Congress, which five years ago said it would

address the issue of pesticide control, now admits it will be at least another ten years before something, if anything, is done.

Ten years from now, at its current rate of decline, the striped bass will no longer roam the inshore waters of the Atlantic from Cape Charles to the St. John. The northeastern migratory striped bass, that creature with its genesis in the great glaciers, will have vanished as a viable species.

Along with Jim, Peter, Ted, and the good friends I fished with during that luminous and tumultuous seven years at the Atlantic's rim, the striped bass will also die.

After that, I am not certain I shall want to live.

ADDENDA AND ACKNOWLEDGMENTS

This is a true book. The chapters about man, about haul-seining, fishing on the East End, are based on my personal experiences as a fisherman there for seven years in the early 1950s. Some details have been changed, some vignettes emphasized to make a point, to tell a story. But the gristle at the center is true, as the story unfolded, when I was there.

I am not a scientist, nor even an academic, so I have not annotated the other chapters: the ones on fish, the striped bass. But I have done considerable research and traveling in preparation for this book. I have documentation and/or direct observation for every statement of fact in these chapters.

But beyond the documentation, beyond my experiences and observations, a host of people have helped with this book — people who, because of their concern for the striper, for all of us, gave their time, their work, their support, their information, their memories, and their encouragement. They must be noted.

On the East End, at the *East Hampton Star*, there is Everett T. Rattray, the editor and publisher of that fine weekly newspaper that pays such attention to the region's commercial fishermen. Two reporters, Susan Pollack and Steven Bromely, at the *Star* produced work I leaned on each week.

Beyond the paper, the Marine Museum near the beach in Amagansett, and Ralph Carpentier, who used to fish with us once in a while, provided me with much help, as the museum director and keeper of the fishing files.

Dudley Roberts, a sportsfisherman of the first order, was helpful to me when the time came to write the Montauk part of the book. Dudley not only took me offshore, but set up a historic fishing trip (the only one of its kind) with the three members of the Pitts brothers: Gus, Ralph and Clancy. Along with mate Ted Sigler, they gave me a rare day under the Light.

Stuart Vorpahl, a good and articulate commercial fisherman, has been a constant resource, generous with his time and equipment. And my oldest friends, Francis Lester and Peter Matthiessen, helped much with the accurate restoration of my memories.

In Maryland, on the Nanticoke and Choptank, I came to know Avis Boyd and Bob Pond — two people who know more about the striped bass, and who fight harder for its survival, than most other people on the East Coast. They introduced me to Joe Boone, the warmhearted, easygoing, but absolutely thorough fisheries biologist who spends so many of his days with the creatures of the Chesapeake. I also owe much to my friend, Maryland Senator Porter Hopkins, who kept me in close touch with bass bulletins, and to William Warner, author of *Beautiful Swimmers* — the definitive book for anyone wanting to know Chesapeake Bay.

Other good and concerned people, like Shaw Mudge in Greenwich, Connecticut, Donal C. O'Brien, Jr., in New York City, Janine Selendy in New Canaan, Connecticut, and Glenn McBay of the U.S. Fish & Wildlife Service in Jackson, Mississippi, went far beyond even the call of friendship and service to send me materials about the striper that I otherwise would never have seen.

Resource material also came from Bruce Rogers and Debbie Weston at the Oceanographic Institute of Rhode Island, and from the Ichthyological Association, Inc., in Ithaca, New York.

I must pay special attention to Robert H. Boyle of *Sports*

Illustrated. His book, *The Hudson River,* is the definitive work on that body of water, and Bob Boyle has quite likely forgotten more about the striped bass than I shall ever learn. He has been fighting for its survival and protection for most of his life. I hope he finds this book a help in those efforts.

Here in Maine, where the book was written, I thank Peter Cox, publisher of *Maine Times,* the newspaper I worked for at the time, for being so patient with my use of the office. The Bowdoin College Library provided generous and valuable assistance, as did my neighbor, Jim McLoughlin, whose library comes close to Bowdoin's in scope, and Arthur Hummer, whose knowledge of the wild is extensive.

Marvin Kuhn, the East End artist, drew the illustrations. Marvin is also a friend, a good one, an old one, from fishing days. He understands this book, and he went far beyond the dimensions of his assignment in his efforts to add such visual grace to its pages. I can only hope the book will help to bring Marvin some of the recognition he has earned.

The best is saved for last. I have been promising my wife Jean for the past several years that I wanted to write a proper book. Now that I have made the effort, I wonder if she wants to hear such issues raised, ever again. I did the writing, but Jean did the typing, the copying, the checking, the telephoning, the pursuing of research, the answering of questions, the orderly assembly of information, and through it all, kept the budgets, the house, the dinner table, and our seven children in such wonderful condition that few worldly problems ever interrupted progress on the book. She is a miracle, and it is she, more than anyone, more than myself, who made this book happen.